Obstacles Equal Opportunities

Volume II

The Enlightened Journey: How 13 Individuals Overcame Obstacles to Create Success in their Lives

Compiled by Heather Andrews

www.heatherandrews.press
www.followitthrupublishing.com
http://www.getyouvisible.com/

Although the author and publisher have made every effort to ensure that the information in this book was correct at press time, the author and publisher do not assume and hereby disclaim any liability to any party due to these words coming from the author's own opinion based on their experiences.

Every word in this book is based on the author's own experience of their personal development journey and the outcomes with clients that they may have witnessed. Although we have made every reasonable attempt to achieve complete accuracy in the content of this book, we assume no responsibility for errors or omissions in the information in this book.

You should only use this information as you see fit at your own risk. Your life and circumstances may not be suited to these examples with what we share within these pages. The author and publisher are neither doctors nor in the position of registered authorities to give you expert advice. All we can share is what we have tested on ourselves and obtained through witnessing the changes in our lives or our clients' lives along the way.

Print ISBN: 9781513649139

Gratitude

First, I want to thank each of the co-authors that contributed to this book for their vulnerability and willingness to share their knowledge. Their stories are powerful, and their wisdom will offer you the path to changing your financial story.

I am grateful to my amazing, publishing team: my editors who help guide and coach our authors through the process of sharing their stories despite their fears. My graphic design team who created the cover and my podcast team for helping our co-authors bring a voice to their story.

I am grateful to you, our readers. Thank you for joining our journey.

Most of all, I am grateful for the lessons I have learned through my finance story. I am glad we are finally bringing the topic of money to the table so we as a society can openly discuss, learn, and grow together for a stronger financial future for ourselves and our community.

Hugs,
Heather

Contents

Foreword

Do you consider yourself resilient? Are you the type of person who emotionally, physically and spiritually bounces back quickly, and is stronger and wiser after misfortune or change?

Are you curious like me and wonder how much of it is due to genetics, the environment or what you do to hone that characteristic?

As a prison physician, I had the unique opportunity of seeing different levels of resilience in individuals, whether they were battling life-threatening disease or facing life imprisonment with no possibility of parole. Resilience has always been important in life, but I feel its importance will heighten in an age where technologic advances become disruptive at an ever-increasing rate.

I'm intrigued with the research done in genetics where certain genes have garnered names, like the 'warrior' or the 'worrier' gene and what they actually do. What's more important though, is how our environment, experiences and choices in life affect the expression of those genes, which we call epigenetics.

Some people love the intricacies of science like I do, but most people just want to know how to build resilience. When I took care of patients who were resilient and beat the death sentence that doctors gave them, I took notice. What they all shared was optimism and hope. That is why when I took care of what appeared to be a terminal patient and they asked me -- "How much time do I have left, Doc?"-- I would first say, "Let me share a story about my husband, Clifton, who was told by doctors that he only had a short time to live when he was 25."

At twenty-five he was a company commander in Vietnam and on Christmas Eve in 1969 he was shot thru the chest collapsing his lung and lacerating one of the coronary arteries feeding his heart.

It was a miracle he ended up in a MASH unit before bleeding out. He spent almost two years in a military hospital watching many men give up the fight and die. He was told that he was a cardiac cripple and if he just stayed in a wheelchair and not strain his heart, he might live a few years. He chose to live his way and pushed himself a little every day to get stronger. He also chose to believe that he would get better and that nothing would stop him. He wasn't afraid of dying. He told me that when he was shot, he wondered if he was going to die, and he said he heard a voice that said, "No, you've got more to do." He became a martial arts competitor, someone who ran a half- marathon, is a bodybuilder and has worked in the business world as a strategist and acted as a teacher and mentor to thousands for the past fifty years. He is still going strong at seventy-five and will be in another bodybuilding contest this year, 2019.

I led with that story to give them hope and to remind them that doctors don't always know the outcome of someone with a serious or a potentially fatal disease. We try to remind ourselves and our patients, that what is important, is WHO has the disease. We ask ourselves if there is some way we can help people be more resilient and be the ones who bounce back and beat the odds.

In this age of information overload, I have found that people tend not to remember what you say, they remember how you make them feel. A well-told story that is relevant, resonates and inspires, or gives them hope, sticks with them. I still remember one of the inmates who told me that it wasn't that I just gave them hope, I gave them the ability to 'practice' it. He was referring to their opportunity to help me run programs that I started in the prison as a volunteer, which ranged from HIV support groups to substance abuse classes. He said that the chance to be of service to someone else, besides being consumed with his own issues made him more resilient in overcoming his own medical and addiction problems.

Resilient people are optimistic and not giving up hope is essential for their success. They also tend to be altruistic or service oriented. When you are trying to bounce back from a major setback, you are more invested in it, if you are also doing it for loved ones or a cause that you are committed to.

In Clifton's case, he had a powerful reason to live, and it was because of his love and commitment to his twelve-year-old brother, Kenny. When Clifton was in the hospital fighting for his life, he found out that his mother was dying, his father was out of the picture and he needed to survive and thrive so he could take care of Kenny. Clifton also shared with me that raising his younger brother helped him overcome his PTSD from the war.

How do you access hope, optimism, and altruism when you are knocked down and don't have it? Some access it externally thru their faith and religious beliefs. Some access it internally by going on their own spiritual journey. Regardless of the approach, it's what we tell ourselves and believe that is the crucial piece.

When Clifton was shot thru the chest and lying in that rice paddy in Vietnam, he said he became calm when he heard the answer to his question, "Am I going to die?" Clifton is not a religious person, but he chose to believe the answer, "No, you've got more to do." Faith-based people would say it was God. People who don't believe in God would say humans always have an internal dialog going on in their head and what's important is what narratives we believe.

Consider these two narratives. One person believes they are worthy, they are lovable, and they have a purpose in life. That is the narrative that Clifton already had in his head due to his upbringing and environment. He was the first born of two educated parents who loved him, had high expectations of him and held him accountable.

Another person believes they are unworthy, not lovable and do not have a purpose in life. That is the narrative that many of the inmates had, because they had the exact opposite experience when they grew up. They did not have two educated parents who loved them. Many just had an uneducated mother who lived at the survival level and was dealing with her own issues like addiction, mental illness, physical and sexual abuse. Their environment did not include family or individuals who had high expectations of them and held them accountable.

If your narrative is that you are unworthy, not lovable, and do not have a purpose in life you tend not to be resilient, unless you recognize your internal dialogue and act to change it. When I was teaching a life skills course in the prison, Tom, an inmate who was 50 and had been placed in prison many times, came up to me and said, "Dr. G., you know, I've been sitting in this class listening to you for the last couple of months and I see you volunteer your time and you actually care about us. It got me thinking. How come I don't care about myself?"

Tom had grown up in a dysfunctional, abusive, uncaring environment, where his older brother started shooting him up with heroin when he was seven years old. When he asked himself that question it was like a light went on. He began to understand that the story of his unworthiness was the result of his experiences in childhood, not his intrinsic worth. He could choose a different story and believe that he was worthy to be cared for and loved. He started to realize that his self-worth was shaped by external factors when he was too young to understand that he did not have to believe what his family told him.

I have found that when you study resilient people you will see at their core, self-worth, optimism, purpose, and a belief in something bigger than just themselves. They also are learners and want to understand which thought systems and activities will help make them become more resilient.

Those activities include adequate sleep, healthy nutrition, appropriate physical activity, meditation and good social connections. Many of us know that those things are important, but we rationalize that we don't have the time, energy or will power to tackle them. Why don't we make them a priority and a habit when our resilience and lives depend on them? I've asked that of myself at different times in my life and come up with a variety of excuses. I know though, that I am at my most resilient when I do all those activities. I also know that when one of those activities truly becomes a habit, I don't have to use my energy on will power.

What one activity can you work on so it becomes a habit? If you don't sleep a good eight hours a night, I would start there. I know many people deprive themselves of sleep because they feel that they have too many things to do, but research shows that if you are rested and do your hardest work when you are the most alert you will do it faster and better. Everyone has a different internal clock where they feel the most alert and energetic. Get in the habit of doing your hardest and most stressful work then.

I look at resilience the same way I look at building a muscle. If you want your resilience to be stronger you need to stress yourself a little at a time, do it consistently and monitor your outcome. That means you have to get out of your comfort zone. When you are in your comfort zone, you don't need resilience. You need resilience when you are far out from your comfort zone. Many of us avoid getting out of our comfort zone because we don't want to deal with rejection, confrontation or things that frighten us.

As an example, many of us say that we dread public speaking because we don't want to appear a fool, be rejected or confronted by people who have a different point of view. As a shy, introvert

I had a hard time getting over my dread of public speaking, but now I enjoy it. It didn't happen overnight. It happened by doing small things first, like teaching the inmates, then medical staff, then custody officers in the prison, speaking at clubs like rotary and eventually giving presentations at a state and national level.

Resilience is also one of those traits that we want to encourage in others, especially children. How do we do that in children? If we protect them too much, make it too easy for them or make excuses for them they will not get out of their comfort zone and will not build up their muscle of resilience. If schools and parents put too much value on grades children will tend to take the easiest road to get them. They won't take advanced placement classes or subjects that do not come easily to them. Children would best be served for awarding their effort and how many times they get up after being knocked down versus doing well in something they have an aptitude for.

Resilience can also be contagious, whether it is in a small group like a family or a large group like an organization. Resilience and its tone is set by the leader and the culture he or she creates. It is demonstrated in the stories and the mythologies they promote and their behavior and ability to teach it to others.

I encourage all of you to be the type of parent or leader that promotes resilience. We will need it more than ever in the decades to come.

Karen Gedney MD, ABAARM
DiscoverDrG.com
Author of '30 Years Behind Bars,' Trials of a Prison Doctor

Introduction

Obstacles. Challenges. Trials.

Whatever you call them, every single one of us has had to overcome something in our lives; be that a physical disadvantage, a financial setback, a business complication, an emotional hurdle, or spiritual snag.

The biggest hurdle in getting through any challenge is not letting it affect the upward trajectory of our success long-term—to move past the disappointment and carry on with a glint in your eye and a shimmy in your step.

And that, my friends, is all about mindset.

Following the highly successful *Obstacles Equal Opportunities,* I'm overjoyed to present *Obstacles Equal Opportunities: Volume II.* I'm thrilled you've chosen to join me and thirteen of my inspiring co-authors as we delve into the topic of overcoming the odds to create successful businesses, relationships and lives.

Throughout this book, we aim to ignite your confidence and your drive to overcome whatever challenge you happen to be up against, with authenticity, vulnerability, and good old-fashioned grit. We also hope to help you expose the humbling wisdom in the lesson, and learn how to change your circumstances by shifting your mindset—*choosing* to win from now on.

You'll also discover how our brave authors learned how to thrive in the face of adversity, as they tackled the obstacles set in front of them and systematically overcame what was holding them back. These powerful personal stories are a testament to the human spirit, and just how resilient we can be when we set our minds to it.

Collectively, we hope you're able to gain insight into how to overcome adversity in your own life, through the sharing of our experiences, in our lessons learned, and in the mindset tips from each co-author.

From a personal standpoint, this book is yet another milestone in the professional evolution of Heather Andrews, which would not have been possible without the challenges I have had thrown my way in the last three years. Every obstacle has been a blessing in disguise.

Win or learn, we just need to keep moving *forward*.

Love,
Heather

Matthew Biggar

Matthew Biggar started out as an entrepreneur at the age of twenty-five when he thought he had it all figured out. It took him nearly a decade of struggling in different businesses and sales jobs before Matthew discovered his purpose and path to a profitable and fulfilling business.

Working the nine to five and spending more money than was coming in put him in a position of losing everything. It was a matter of swallowing his pride and moving back home with his parents or becoming homeless.

This led to a decision to change his life and discover a new world where he could inspire people to seek their true potential.

Today Matthew loves working with heart-centric entrepreneurs who are motivated to create a legacy built on growth, abundance and transformation.

Connect with Matthew:
https://empoweringvideo.com

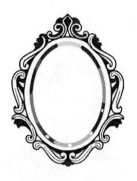

Chapter 1

When You Feel Stuck, Look in the Mirror

By Matthew Biggar

I was trying to understand why I was experiencing so much resistance when contemplating my life so far. Like everyone, I had faced some challenges, but that didn't explain the intensity of my negative feelings. I didn't know it at the time, but it had everything to do with my mindset and my attitudes towards money and relationships. That initial questioning, however, started me down a path of exploration. It took me on a journey of discovery that would change my life. I would learn that my own beliefs and behavior patterns were the real obstacles to my success.

As I considered my own situation, I noticed that there were plenty of other people who had succeeded in completely transforming themselves. They had gone from a life of struggle and failure to one of success and fulfillment. Change occurred more quickly for some than for others, but they all got there eventually. My question was, "What makes them different?" Why had they succeeded where others had failed?

As I pondered these questions, I became fascinated with the idea of learning more about money and business. I read everything I could find on these subjects and, in the process, discovered more positive ways of thinking about them. My true awakening, however, occurred when I began my entrepreneurial journey. That's when I became aware that, when it came to money, my belief system was all messed up. I had terrible money habits. And so began the process of my re-education.

Hovering near bankruptcy and in danger of becoming homeless, I decided to make a change. Thinking that I would find all the answers I needed in books, I headed down to the local bookstore. I basically expected to find a set of instructions to follow, but I found so much more than that. A whole new world opened up for me, changing my perspective on how to achieve success. I learned that I didn't have to work a "9-to-5" job to succeed in life. Instead, I could start a business and live by a different set of rules as a business owner.

A friend of mine once said, "Once you become aware, there's no going back. There's no hiding from it." I made the decision to face my demons head-on, with full awareness. I proceeded with an open mind and, whenever a new challenge appeared, I would take it up with eyes wide open. I would put in whatever time was necessary to overcome it. I knew that changing my beliefs around money and developing a new mindset would not happen overnight, but I knuckled down and did the work.

For the next ten years, I continued to work at corporate sales jobs, but all of my spare time was spent reading books from the business section at Chapters.

At one point, I came across an online job posting asking for help with videography. I literally had no idea what I was doing, but I loved technology and photography. I am the type of guy that raises his hand and says, "Hey, I can help you with that," and then I go figure out how to do it. That's what I did in this case.

I remember sitting down at the computer and trying to figure out how the editing software worked. For some reason, I got discouraged very quickly. I didn't know how to put the project together. I took myself out of the game right away. It was *too hard,* so I quit. The problem was that I didn't have the mindset required to push through challenges, not until many years later.

I couldn't let go of the idea of working with video, however, and continued to pursue the idea. Once that camera was in my hands, I realized that I was very much a kinesthetic learner. I wasn't built for school because it lacked the practical, physical experience I needed to learn. But, making videos was so hands-on that I was able to quickly grasp the basics.

That's when I realized how complex production really is. I would need to develop expertise in many areas in order to authentically tell someone else's story and do it justice.

I fell in love with the power of video and how it creates opportunities for connecting with people on a deeply emotional level. Its creative potential for telling any story imaginable was intoxicating. The more I thought about it, the more I wanted to do it. I really wanted to create videos that I was proud of.

I made a lot of mistakes along the way, but I learned from them. The most important lesson came from the money side of the business and how my mindset was sabotaging my success. I was spending too much money buying tools I thought I needed to build a profitable business. At first, it was easy to explain away the spending as an investment, but it quickly became more like an addiction masquerading as a solution. I can't tell you how many times I bought equipment that didn't work out, that wasn't what I needed, and that ended up being a total waste of money. To make matters worse, I then took a second hit when I resold my new purchases at a loss.

I was filling a void instead of looking at the person in the mirror. The only one holding me back was me. I went through a long process of self-discovery and personal growth before realizing that I had limiting beliefs around self-worth, and was afraid of being judged. All of these feelings and subconscious beliefs were intertwined with my attitudes toward money and how I valued my own services. Once I became aware of my limiting beliefs and dealt with them, I was able to adjust my mindset and make better business decisions.

Like many new business owners, I had gotten caught up in appearances rather than substance. As Gary Vaynerchuck would say, "people try to be fancy when they're not fancy". I decided to refocus my efforts on the needs of my customers. I wanted to understand them better, get to know them on a deeper level, and come up with creative, transformative solutions to their problems.

I knew that anyone could create quality videos with basic, inexpensive equipment. Delivering a good product that met the needs of my customers and exceeded their expectations was the best way for me to ensure my success. Today, my clients are business owners who want to leverage the power of video to grow their personal brand, increase their income, or create impactful change for other people. The challenge is that they are too close to their own brand to simplify and clarify their message in a way that attracts their ideal customer. That's where I come in.

Initially, I wasn't sure what niche I should target with my business. Who did I want to work with? I felt that the power of video and story, if misused, would be like handing over a powerful weapon to a villain. So, I heavily filtered out customers and failed to position my brand effectively.

I eventually decided that, for me, finding the right niche not only meant having a steady supply of paying customers, but the work also had to be personally rewarding.

Initially, I invested $26,000 in a business coach and rushed into creating a real estate video business because I thought following the coach's advice was all I would need to feel successful. After a year of filming empty houses, I realized that real estate video really wasn't doing it for me; it wasn't fulfilling. So, I killed off that brand and started Empowering Video. I wanted to work with heart-centric people and tell their stories in creative ways. I wanted to help them share their message in a way that would help them grow their business and attract their ideal customer.

That still wasn't enough for me. I was obsessed with finding ways to bring more value to my customers and to the world.

I took a leap of faith and quit my job, which was terrifying because my fears around money and security were stilling controlling me. I started to work on myself. I began replacing my negative beliefs with positive ones that served me better and allowed for the future I envisioned for my family.

At the age of thirty-five, I started to think in terms of my legacy. I decided that the best way to leave a positive mark on this world was to embrace abundance, and I redoubled my efforts to get a handle on my inner game. As I became more aware of my relationship with the person in the mirror, I began peeling back the layers of my internal struggle. The work paid off, and I was able to develop new thoughts, feelings, and beliefs built on abundance rather than scarcity. I was now in a position to make better choices about how I wanted to show up for people.

Over time, I began to understand that if I was struggling in an area, it was usually a symptom of a deeper resistance within me. In his book, *The Success Principles,* Jack Canfield taught me to take 100 percent responsibility for everything in my life, and so I did. Sometimes it took more than one try. I would tackle an issue and feel like I was flipping a switch, only to later realize that I still had more work to do when it resurfaced in another form. It was not always easy, but it was rewarding each time I overcame a limiting belief pattern.

Working on my mindset is what has made the biggest difference in my life. When I became more aware of how my subconscious worked, I was able to effectively address the limiting beliefs that were holding me back. Simply put, I didn't have enough confidence in myself, I was afraid of being judged by people, and I had self-worth issues. My beliefs affected every aspect of my life, from my personal relationships to my professional success.

Once I became aware, I was able to take action. It became a matter of figuring out what resources, people, mentors, coaches, influences, and collaborators I should let into my life to resolve these issues more quickly.

As it turns out, videography is a roller coaster business. It's an up and down ride. There's a big difference between being a creative technician and being a business *owner*. Once I became a business owner, I was responsible for everything: growth, income, and impact in the world. It was very daunting. What I needed was to build a community of collaborators who were on a similar path to my own, so I wouldn't have to go it alone. There just weren't enough hours in the day to do everything myself, especially if I wanted to grow the business.

You know when you *get* people and they *get* you? And, how that makes working together even more amazing? I think everybody wants that kind of collaborative chemistry in their personal and professional relationships. I knew that I couldn't do it alone, but I was still struggling with my message and how to reach the right people.

Most of us want to help people. It's in our nature. It's rewarding and it makes a difference. I believe humanity has a purpose and that everyone should be on a journey to find their own way. You get to choose your own path, so consider what might be holding you back. We'll never have all of the answers, but that doesn't mean we shouldn't strive to reach our full potential. Isn't that the point of being alive?

I was definitely doing better but I still wasn't always reaching for that highest potential. I was holding back. I was playing small. That's when I decided to make my first video about my business and what motivates me. The message covered why I was here, why I had chosen to work in video, and why I got out of bed at 5 o'clock in the morning to work on my business. I wanted to inspire people.

For so long, I had let fear of judgment and lack of self-worth hold me back from speaking up for myself in my own medium. No more. I finally decided to break free. Shooting that first video was great, but it wasn't enough. One video wasn't going to cut it. I had to make it a habit. I had to become comfortable with speaking for myself on camera. It was difficult at first, but eventually it became second nature.

The only way to overcome the personal challenges that were staring me down like vultures in the desert was to look at the person in the mirror and ask questions like, "What has really been holding you back? What's the source of the struggle? Is it internal or external?" Then, secure in the knowledge that I had the answers within me, all I had to do was wait, listen, and take action.

There's so much that no one tells you about being a successful entrepreneur working on your own. I still had a lot to learn but at least I knew *why* I was doing what I was doing, and that was all that mattered at that moment.

As discussed earlier, it is difficult to do everything all by yourself. In fact, I don't think anyone has ever achieved success totally on their own. Everyone has received some kind of help along the way from mentors, partners, and collaborators. Nothing exists in a vacuum.

I had always heard that networking was one of the best ways to meet people and that it was essential for building success, but it seemed to me that it could easily become a numbers game. I wanted to cultivate real relationships and I felt that ordinary networking just wasn't going to work for me. Thankfully, that didn't mean that I had to do everything by myself. I had other options; I just didn't know it yet.

No one told me that, instead of "networking", I should be building a community of *collaborators,* but that's what felt right to me. So, I started focusing on building more meaningful relationships with people rather than going for superficial connections. As I worked on my own self-acceptance and began to understand the internal growth that needed to happen within me, I was able to show up better and deliver more value to the heart-centric entrepreneurs I was working with.

Self-confidence was a major stumbling block for me. I used to get all kinds of advice from all kinds of people, until a friend of mine said something that stuck. He told me that I already had all of the tools that I needed to succeed and that it kind of pissed him off that I didn't seem to recognize my own potential. I realized that I needed to stop asking everyone and instead seek out the advice of people who had gotten results where I wanted to succeed.

I kept receiving this message in different ways. A year later, another friend also noted my lack of self-confidence. The truth was that my personal development practices did not seem to be helping me enough to achieve real success, because I didn't yet understand the depth of internal work that was required of me. I didn't understand what was holding me back until I realized that I was relying so much on so many different coaches, mentors, friends, and business owners that I was having a hard time making decisions for myself.

When you can find people who have achieved the results you want, and whose values are aligned with yours, modeling them can be a powerful formula for success. It can be very helpful to understand how they got to where they are. That being said, in the end, you must still make the best decision for you. Trust your gut, no matter what.

I needed to be more selective in my relationships and even more so when it came to taking advice. I wanted to collaborate but I also had to trust myself and my judgment. This lesson was essential to my growth and to the breakthroughs I experienced in all of my relationships.

Believing in yourself also opens doors to new opportunities. When you believe in yourself you are more willing to take risks, try new things, explore new passions, speak to new audiences, and make adjustments where necessary. When you trust your gut, you are more likely to recognize when a change is needed and when it isn't. You also don't feel that you need to hang on to methods and ideas that no longer serve you or your audience. You can sense when a change might soon be warranted and prepare for it. You can also take a leap of faith when the moment is right for you.

One of my mentors helped me a lot by suggesting that I ask myself better questions, such as how do I want to show up in the world? What do I want to bring to the table when I meet someone new? How did I want to interact with people? And, what did I need to learn in order to add more value?

That last one was a biggie. I became obsessed with the idea of offering more value to the people I serve. Investing in myself meant that I could create more value for others; I could become the "servant leader" Jim Collins talked about in his book *Good to Great*. For me, that meant helping my clients with their message and producing transformative video courses for them that would reach their audiences on a powerful, emotional level.

So, to summarize, when I started asking better, more powerful questions, I began to get better and more powerful answers, which led to better, more powerful results. But it didn't happen overnight. It took over ten years for me to figure out how to create the life I wanted, and how to get the results I knew I was capable of. I traveled a tough, all consuming, lonely, and often chaotic road before I finally emerged on the other side and really understood the lessons that life was trying to teach me.

It didn't have to be that way; I could have found better mentors and had more guidance earlier. But, that lonely journey was, in itself, a product of my scarcity mindset. I couldn't see the possibilities or take advantage of better options because I was blind to them. It wasn't until I understood this dynamic that my reality truly began to shift for the better.

Once I gave up my scarcity mindset:

I generated more positive energy. You can too.

I overcame (sometimes self-created) challenges that prevented me from growing. You can too.

I built (and continue to build) the types of relationships I wanted in my life. You can too.

I began to seek my true potential. You can too.

I learned how to look at the person in the mirror to get unstuck. You can too.

Lessons Learned:

1) Choose Your Mentors Carefully: Be selective about who you go to for advice. Pick mentors you can model, people who have succeeded in your area. Don't be proud, be willing to ask for mentorship, and be respectful of their time.

2) Trust Your Instincts: The final decision is always yours. No matter what advice you get, trust your gut, rely on your own intuition. If you agree with the advice, take it; if not, don't. You won't always get it right but nobody does, no matter how successful they are. In the end, success depends on being willing to take risks and trusting your own judgment.

3) Focus on What You Love: It's important to follow your heart, too. If you're doing what you love, you'll be able to meet inevitable challenges and you'll do it willingly. I didn't know anything about video production, but I overcame many obstacles and acquired the skills I needed because I loved what I was doing and wanted to succeed at it, no matter what.

Mindset Tips:

1) Awareness Is Everything: when you are aware of something you can take action. In my case, once I started taking a deeper look at the person in the mirror, I was able to change my limiting beliefs to empowering ones. If you feel stuck, notice where the resistance is. That's the beginning of awareness and change.

2) Self-Confidence Is Power: In order to trust your gut, you must have a strong sense of self and be confident in your decisions. Mistakes are inevitable; everybody makes them. You need to have the confidence to trust yourself anyway. If you want mutual respect and strong relationships in all areas, self-confidence is the key.

3) Show Up with Abundance Not Scarcity: a scarcity mindset is what holds most people back. When you open up to sharing yourself with the world, abundance begins to flow to you in equal or greater measure. That's when everything starts moving forward at speed, and you can begin to realize your true potential.

Aha Moments and Self Reflection

Note your Thoughts

Todd Boyum

Todd Boyum is the president of Reach Me Global, a coaching, training, and consulting firm located near Austin, Texas. He is a Certified High-Performance Coach and founder of the Faith Performance Network.

Todd discovered his faith in God and love of personal development at the same time: the start of his adult life and career. Together, these two continuous pursuits have guided him during his leadership in the army, thirty years as a technology leader at Dell, dozens of leadership roles in churches and volunteering with the Boy Scouts of America.

Todd, and his wife, Cheryl, have eight grown children and eight grandchildren.

Connect with Todd:

www.toddboyum.com

www.facebook.com/ToddBoyum/

www.instagram.com/toddboyum/

Chapter 2

Guiding Altars at the Mountain Pass

By Todd Boyum

"Set it up. I'm totally ready to have this conversation with HR."

The delay in my manager's response told me he was hesitant. "You know," I sighed, "I feel like I'm playing a therapist role for management and HR here. I'm the one that requested the change, and I'm ready to go, so please, set up the meeting so we can move this forward. I appreciate your concern, but the worst part for me is that we're continuing to stay in limbo month after month. Let's go."

This was a conversation I was having with my boss of seven years. He understood the background completely. Two days later, we were preparing to walk into a meeting with HR for an hour. They were concerned that there was something strange happening. Employees don't typically request to step out of management and be demoted. They wanted to make sure I was truly okay —make sure it wasn't coming back on them somehow.

I just wanted to grab lunch with one of my employees and was confident that the issue could be addressed in less than ten minutes. I was resolved and peaceful about stepping down— but the reason had more to do with the fact that I was hungry, had already made my decision, and now wanted to focus on other parts of my plan that needed attention, during this lunch meeting.

The HR rep stated the situation as he understood it. I told him, "It's true. In September, I formally requested to return to an individual contributor position for personal reasons. Now, apparently, management desires that I lower my grade too. This doesn't change anything for me. As stated in the email I sent back in September, I need more work-life balance to focus on some challenges going on in my personal life."

Dutifully, the HR rep proceeded to point out that, while my pay would not decrease, it would now be at the top of my new pay scale, so I might have a hard time ever receiving a raise again. I assured him I understood.

Stacking upon his first warning, he added it might be difficult for future managers to understand my decision to get out of management. I wanted to accelerate through these speed-bumps in his mind so, I pressed the gas through his warnings saying, "I can see that, especially since I'm taking a step down, too." His eyes opened wider, and I could tell I added a point he had not considered. Seeing the opportunity to cruise through the finish line, I unswervingly added, "I guess I'll just have to deal with that when the time comes." My effort succeeded, and the HR rep said, "Okay, good."

He offered to make the change at the beginning of the next pay period, but my boss told him they weren't quite ready to do that yet as there were some delays in the reorganization plan, so they'd let him know when. We agreed to leave the timing open as we left the room exactly ten minutes after the meeting started.

It's true I requested to step down in September. To be completely honest, while I was making that decision to accomplish things I wanted, it was also necessary to do so, because I found myself in an unexpectantly hostile environment. Earlier that year, our team was reorganized underneath a vice president who almost immediately began to devalue our team, focusing specifically on me and a few others. He began a campaign to push me out of the organization even though I had always been a top performer and despite the amazing value my team and I had created for our company.

This was infuriating and hurtful to me at first. I'd dedicated a tremendous amount of my life to our company and my team and had been very successful, yet none of that seemed to matter. It felt very unfair and clearly personal. But I was fortunate for many reasons. I had a great track record, the support of my manager and team as well as others at work. The real secret weapon though was that I had my own plan.

I knew before my VP took over our team that a shift was on the horizon for me. I'd already accomplished what I set out to do—build a game-changing product that was not only positively impacting our company but also our industry. I developed a high-performance team, and I felt a lot of personal fulfillment. It was the largest thing I'd ever achieved at a company that I had been employed with for thirty years—my personal magnum opus.

What I know about myself is that I need bigger challenges—things that grow me the way my heart longs to grow. I know that is not always, or even usually, how others measure success. It didn't seem possible or desirable for me to take on something bigger than this program in a global corporate environment in the future.

My work environment had slowly deteriorated over the last few years. Like a frog in warm water, lulled into a trance before the boil, I had become numb to how much it was impacting me physically while returning decreasing dividends.

There was a time we were firing on all cylinders. We had great management that understood what we were accomplishing, a great program and a great team. We were doing future-oriented, impactful programs. We were learning. It was a lot of fun, and people around the company were excited about what we were accomplishing.

However, all good things come to an end. Nothing and I knew it was only a matter of time before leadership changes and other factors would begin to shift our work from spirited innovation and passionately pioneered_________, to more tactical, operational efficiency. We had a great run—keeping all cylinders intact, but over the last couple years, things begin to change—the way that programs change when they start to become the status quo themselves because they've achieved their initial launch and growth.

I'd been thinking during these last two years about what was next as I knew it was time to move on. But I loved my team, and I loved what we were doing. I wasn't really in a hurry, and nothing was appearing on the horizon that drew me to a different course.

I remembered an interesting insight from a conference speaker about God creating us in His image. In the Genesis account, before God says, "Let there be light," it says:

> *The earth was without form and void, and darkness was over the face of the deep. And the Spirit of God was hovering over the face of the waters.*

This speaker pointed out that people sometimes need to hover over the unformed and unclear dreams of their life before making future decisions. That's what I'd been doing for the previous few years—hovering over this moment, waiting, looking, examining what God wanted next for me.

Should I try to do something else at this company or move on? Should I try to work for a smaller company? Should I pick up this dream God had given me nearly ten years ago? These questions swirled in those murky waters in my soul.

Late in 2017, God stirred that dream back up in my heart. I began to see that it was time to set aside corporate America and pursue a message that God had given me to take the world. The clarity of vision reawakened in my soul was almost simultaneously accompanied by shifts and changes in my work life. They were annoying and frustrating at the beginning, but I began to see them as good omens signaling I was on the right path.

Sometimes, the obstacles we have are the ones we create for ourselves. It is hard to decrease and let others increase, especially when we love something. Men tend to get their identity caught up with their work. I long ago learned to separate the two, but I must admit I was finding I was not completely free of that illusion. I was too wrapped up in my work. Even though I decided to move towards my future dream, I knew I would have had a difficult time backing away from my current work. Fortunately, God provided a catalyst in the form of this VP who did not want me on his team.

He was trying to force my boss to force me to take a position in a different part of the company. I didn't really want to change positions. I'd already made up my mind that I would retire from corporate America the following year. I didn't like the idea of telling a different leader that I would come in and do something great for them, knowing I planned to leave in the next eight months. Furthermore, there was work I wanted to complete in my current position.

In early January, before all this had started, I was meeting with my coach. She asked me how I would find the time and energy to pursue my transition while sustaining my current work? "Todd," she asked, "How will you finish well?"

There were two things that came to mind. First, I needed to help my team be successful even after I was gone. Second, I needed to focus my energy on my management responsibilities and less on our product development – which would let my top performer grow and be seen more while freeing me up to recover my energy for my future.

Many times, in my past work and volunteering, I had learned a practical lesson from John the Baptist's statement about Jesus. "He must increase, but I must decrease." My team was already performing to a high standard and no longer needed my direct help driving the product portfolio. However, they did need me to help position them as the future management team to continue these programs after I left. Securing them as the future management team was the definition of finishing things well, as far as I was concerned.

My wife, Cheryl, and I attended a conference in Phoenix in September, then celebrated our anniversary by visiting the Grand Canyon. While at the conference, I seriously considered coming back from vacation and resigning. It would mean losing significant income from bonuses and long-term incentives that I would receive before my planned departure. These funds would help sustain us as we grew our business together, but I was unsure if I could stay in that frustrating and hostile environment that long.

While hiking the Grand Canyon, I was reminiscing about a hike with Gary up Mt. Phillips, the second highest mountain at Philmont. Our sons were in Boy Scouts together, and we were chaperoning the group. Mount Phillips was not much lower than the highest mountain—just enough to allow for overnight camps instead of day hikes but staying overnight had some challenges that required preparation.

We'd be well above the waterline, so the main challenge was taking extra water up the mountain, as it would be at least noon the next day before we would find usable water again. We dispersed half of Gary's gear to the team's pack, enabling him to carry five gallons of water on his back.

He'd had knee surgery before, so he hiked the trail slowly with measured steps. One comical aspect of our journey was watching the younger scouts sprinting up the mountain, exhausting themselves and stopping. Gary would slowly catch up and pass them then they would run and pass him again. It was very much like the tortoise and the hare story all the way to the top.

As we were coming to the peak, Gary and I observed we were at the halfway point in our journey. If he'd gotten hurt, it was just as far to go back as to go forward. In real journeys, these are your options—unlike in modern life, sometimes we choose illusions and distractions when the going gets tough.

Remembering this conversation, I realized I could take the seemingly easier solution and quit now, or I could advance the adventure on my own terms. I hadn't completed what I wanted to finish well, and we still had to prepapre for our future business. Besides, the struggle is part of the journey.

This entire obstacle with my VP had been a journey in itself. It started with critiques about minor communication skills I needed to improve. While sharper than I'd heard before, they weren't new, so I had no issue agreeing that I could improve in these areas, and committed to the work. What was different was his threats that I would have to leave the group if I couldn't address these concerns. He said I could work to turn the situation around, but it soon became clear he'd already made up his mind and wanted me to move on.

Since communications and human relations is an ongoing personal study of mine, I decided to focus on improving my skills irrespective of his intentions. I conducted many interviews with other leaders and coworkers to learn more. While this was helping me improve myself, it was also becoming very clear from these conversations that there was much more involved. This helped me make sense of what seemed like a wildly out of proportion response to what everyone defined as minor soft skills challenges.

I learned that concerns about the organization were centered on me because I had been the spokesman for our products. Some leaders expressed these activities as a lack of support from executive leadership who had asked me to drive this program, but did not give me the support necessary to succeed. Many other surprising insights surfaced as well. It became clear to me the bigger deficit in my skills was my limited understanding of the political nature in my corporate environment.

Learning all this was helpful because it completely solidified my confidence in myself—independent of my achievements or the circumstances at that moment. I was hard on myself at the beginning, but now I could see that it was much more the result of the organization's ineffectiveness, and a clear reminder of what I wanted and did not want in my future life. In other words, I was completely on course.

It helped my wife, and I define how we wanted our business culture to be in the future, providing a contrasting guard rail that we wanted to stay away from. While I learned many things in my career that would serve us well in our business, we also wanted to avoid the realities resident in most corporate environments that would not be helpful for us or our clients. Consequently, much of the envisioning of our business and how we would work and live together in the future became much clearer than it would've been if we had not gone through these experiences.

One of the great things I learned from others in my interviews was that executive leaders usually have other motivations when they are trying to move people out of their organization. As I continued my interviews, it became obvious my VP wanted to grow his leadership team by putting in place his own choices, but was unable to secure the number of positions at the grade he wanted. His motivation was to reclaim those positions from people he didn't want on his team.

As I stared out on the vast Grand Canyon observing the power of God, I knew who I was and what God was doing. I could simply separate myself from the junk at my company and from my own ego and move my goals forward.

I calculated that if I took myself out of the line of fire by getting out of management and, even if necessary, taking a demotion, I could continue to make the same income and acquire my bonus as planned. I could then set myself up to focus on helping the team gain leadership positions, while simultaneously freeing myself up to focus more on my future. It would decrease my weight of responsibility of people and administrative tasks, and allow me to work from home more, all of which would give me more mental bandwidth.

Descending back and forth between the switchbacks of the Grand Canyon and witnessing the changing vistas above and below, reminded me of the journey down from Mount Phillips with my friend, Gary. It's sometimes hard to make sense of the progress you're making. You can see the summit or valley and sense your progress at some points on the trail, but brush and rock formations obscure them at other times. You must have faith, and trust that if you are moving forward, you are indeed making progress, even though you can't see it.

I thought, *That's true, I'm the kind of person who knows how to manage much more complicated situations on my own terms and God has faithfully helped me in all those times, so He would surely help me here too.*

The last time I felt another person had seriously impacted my dreams and goals was ten years ago. I discovered that my wife at the time wanted to pursue a different life without me after twenty-five years of marriage. It was a bit shocking and not at all what I wanted. Though we spent a year in counseling, she still made the decision to end our marriage. It felt like a huge betrayal to me not to mention the relationship loss. It also represented the loss of a major dream, which was to never have my children experience their parents' divorce.

During our counseling time, a friend suggested I give my wife an ultimatum. I loved her and didn't feel that would be appropriate or effective. I did need to deal with the reality of what was happening. I knew that whether my wife decided to continue our relationship or not—this rift had been a train wreck in our marriage. It was Gary that had used that analogy in the past. He said, "You might survive, but you must deal with the reality that life is never going to be like it was before the wreck. You're going to have to build a new relationship either way."

I decided to write out who I wanted to be in either situation. If my wife stayed, who would I be in terms of loving and forgiving her and building our future life together? If she chose to depart, who would I be so I could show my children that their father still loved their mother even if we couldn't be together? Also, how would I partner with her in the future to raise our children even though we would no longer share a life together? And as for me—I loved being married and serving my wife and family, and I was not going to become a man that never loved and trusted again. These intentions were pivotal for me.

This pre-examination gave me tremendous clarity and focus when my ex-wife ultimately decided to pursue a divergent life. It guided me in how to honor our past life together as I helped my children cope, showing them how to be strong in deep grief, how to be and feel, proud of the way I handled the biggest disappointment in my life. It became a beacon on how to fearlessly and faithfully love again when Cheryl came into my life.

Now I found myself in this similar place but on a less challenging mountain. I could see the summit against the sky and the dark valley below, so I determined who I would be regardless of the other factors on the landscape, then wrote out my own success scenario despite the obstacles in front of me. The plan included:

1) Giving myself as much freedom and time as possible.
2) Maintaining my current income and financial structure regardless of title/position.
3) Remaining in my organization to support my team's success and to avoid expending energy to learn a new role.
4) Successfully positioning my high-performance team members as leaders in the coming organizational change.

I felt like I could exit gracefully if I could accomplish these goals. When I returned to work, that's exactly what I requested and how it has transpired.

Getting over my ego enabled me to do the right thing for myself, and for others. While staying was uncomfortable, it better served everybody's goals, even the VP in question, and gave me time to realize strengths and lessons that I would not have learned if I was unwilling to go through this misty path on the mountain trail.

As things turned out, I did get clear from most of my leadership responsibilities which gave me the freedom I hoped for. Two of my high-performance team members were promoted into the leadership roles they deserved. The VP's behavior caused other leaders to leave our team because they felt they would not be successful as a result of his leadership. This required me to stay in management at my current grade to manage a small part of my team who no longer had a leader. All the while, as this was occurring, my wife and I continued to establish our future business, taking the time and focus we needed.

Often, the lessons we learn through struggling are how we discover our truest selves. They prepare us to climb higher mountains. It is the drama and cliffhangers at the end of the first act that makes us return to experience the second act. As we look back at all we have learned and the progress we've made, we start this new climb, with wonder in our hearts at what we will experience in our second act. It's going to be awesome.

Lessons Learned

1) It wasn't enough to pursue what I was called to do. I needed to creatively consider who, how, and when as well. Creating a business that duplicated my corporate career lifestyle would have been a disaster. It was just as important to me to include my wife in this dream; our lifestyle needs and our timing.

2) I learned to recognize what God is doing for me, both internally and externally. What may seem like loss is often what's needed to move us faster to our goal. Choosing to look at the experience while detached from my personal feelings enabled me to see it as an elegant catalyst for change, freeing me to partner with it to super charge the impact.

3) Translate integrated success. I recognized I had skills and past experiences that guided me in this challenge.

Mindset Tips

1) Find your authentic self and establish your confidence in who you are. This will enable you to move boldly, based on yourself, irrespective of your situations and circumstances.

2) Don't bring your current environment's limitation into your future, best experience. Design and tailor your dream to what you want, not what you have known and now perceive as 'normal'. True high performance is succeeding beyond standard norms, over the long haul, and without sacrificing your relationships or well-being.

3) Build new community to gain social learning, proof, and support. Most people in your existing circles will not take the new journey with you. Discover who will, and develop a new community early on.

Aha Moments and Self Reflection

Note your Thoughts

Joanna Brown

As a holistic nutrition consultant, natural nutrition clinical practitioner, transformational weight-loss and wellness coach, raw food chef, and corporate wellness specialist, with a Bachelor's Degree in Community and Health Studies, Joanna helps others develop a holistic approach to health and wellbeing. She is a leading whole-living educator, mental health expert, blogger and successful multipreneur helping busy people achieve balance.

Joanna works collaboratively with her clients to free their mind, fuel their body and feed their soul through her one-on-one customized programs and online courses to regain balance, reclaim health, and rejoice in the most vibrant body possible.

Growing up in a household impacted by mental health and addictions, then suffering from her own health crisis due to a lack of balance, fueled her multiple business ventures and advocacy work within the system. Thanks to her resilient spirit and passion for change Joanna is making a positive impact in the lives of others.

Connect with Joanna:

https://rejoicenutritionwellness.com/homepage

https://www.facebook.com/rejoicenutritionwellness/

https://www.instagram.com/rejoicenutritionwellness/

Chapter 3

Rising from the Ashes

By Joanna Brown

"You are Wonder Woman!" people would always say to me. Working over 80 hours a week running a business, being a mom of two active children, cooking everything from scratch, doing every DIY home project you can think of, and finding time to work out while making it all look so easy in the process, earned me numerous titles such as "Wonder Woman", "Lady Boss", and "Super Mom". I proudly wore those labels like badges of honor received in exchange for my blood, sweat, and tears; until, one day, I realized what they had cost me, all of the scars they had left, and all of the sacrifices I had made. Sadly, they were not worth celebrating, and they did they did not serve my overall wellness.

Unfortunately, when we're not doing okay and we need to slow down, we often disregard the subtle cues that our mind and body send out to encourage us to change course. We ignore them until our body gets tired of the abuse and declares, "That's it. I'm shutting down." That is exactly what my body did, and that's when I knew it was time to make some drastic changes if I wanted to survive.

I was adopted and I grew up in a household with a parent that suffered from bi-polar depression, alcoholism, and addictions. This meant that each morning, I would start my day listening to the heavy footsteps coming up from his basement bedroom, waiting and wondering. Who was coming up those stairs? His mood would often dictate how that day would go for everyone living in the house.

As a child, my default was to be angry at the cards I had been dealt. My older brother, a young teenager with a learner's permit, moved quickly into the role of "responsible adult". He got groceries, drove me to swimming lessons, and took us to all the places that we needed to go. He was often told that he would, "need to take care of Joanna when she is older to make sure she doesn't live on the streets." It was stated as harmless joke, but it lived with me for years. Expectations were pretty low that I would ever achieve or amount to anything much in life. Based on my behavior, it was somewhat understandable.

I later focused my anger on the mental health system for its lack of support. The idea that we, the "family", should be the primary caregivers and should shoulder the burden, without any support or resources, fueled my fire. I learned at a very young age that you had to advocate and fight in the system if you wanted any support for those suffering with mental illness and addictions.

Eventually I turned my passion into a career. Working full-time, I put myself through university and obtained my Bachelor's of Community Rehabilitation and Health Studies degree. I was a trail blazer right out of the gate, working to make changes within the current system. This made me popular with some and not so popular with others. One particular consultant took notice of my passion for justice and change, and together we began running a 5-year research project for the provincial government. We worked with people living with dual diagnosis and their families. The idea was that we would not use traditional rehabilitation models. Instead, we used human rights and wholistic approaches to support those with dual diagnosis and their families, who had nowhere else to turn.

The research project quickly grew into a community-based organization with over 100 community members. Today, over a decade later, the community is still learning, evolving, and working to build a world where everyone is a valued citizen. We received enquiries from all over the world asking how we were doing what we were doing. For its part, the government was very interested in how we were improving people's lives and achieving these outcomes at a lower cost than if we had applied traditional models. After four years, we knew we were on to something, but that something was taking its toll on our health and our families, as well.

To successfully get this community-based organization off the ground, my colleague and I had to be on-call 24 hours a day, 7 days a week, 365 days a year. This meant 2:00 a.m. phone calls from suicidal people who needed to be literally talked off a ledge. It also meant that my phone inevitably rang when I was in the middle of reading a favorite bedtime story to my two-year-old daughter. I would have to put the book down and go stand in my laundry room for hours on the phone, while I counseled a crying mother. I shudder to think of the number of books I left half-read on my daughter's bedside table during those first four years. Precious years I would never get back.

But not answering that crisis call was like turning my back on other children and families like the one I grew up in, one that never had anyone to call for help. I knew it was a personal trigger for me, but I couldn't let it happen to someone else like it happened to us. How could I abandon them? I would then make sure to make it up to my daughter any way I could, which meant very little sleep and a constant need to do it all and be perfect in other areas of life.

There were over-the-top birthday parties and special Sunday baking dates in the kitchen with the kids, even on just two hours of sleep. This was when those "Wonder Woman" labels began to flood in. How could I maintain my work schedule and still bring elaborate homemade themed cupcakes to school events? And where did I find the time to build a pink bookshelf for my daughter's bedroom with no days off? Was I some kind of super hero? Or, was it parental guilt? The ugly truth of it was that guilt and manic sleeplessness were at the root of my compensating behavior. What else would drive me to bake and decorate cupcakes at 4:00 a.m. on a Tuesday morning so my kid could take them to school?

Everyone around me, however, seemed to marvel at everything I was able accomplish, so I felt like I must have been doing something right. I wore those labels like a newly minted identity and kept pushing through the mess no one else saw. I did that until my body realized that my stubborn head and heart would never quit and pulled the emergency brake to shut down that non-stop ride.

Third time's the charm.

After four years of that perfectionist work ethic, fueled mainly by my childhood trauma; new parent guilt, and a healthy, daily dose of adrenaline to keep going, my body finally began to shut down over a 6-month period.

The first sign of the shutdown was severe abdominal pains that landed me with a diagnosis of a bleeding ulcer. The changes I made were small, like dropping one or two teams at work and reducing my coffee intake. The second sign came a few months later; it was Thanksgiving and my partner's uncle had passed away. His whole family was coming down for the funeral. Naturally, I offered to host dinner for everyone. Of course, I overdid it *all*, as I always did.

I put on a Thanksgiving dinner with name cards and all the trimmings that would have put Martha Stewart to shame.

I had not been feeling great for a few weeks, but I ignored the signals for a little while longer. Dinner went well, and they all decided to continue the party at another family member's home. Not feeling so great, I chose to stay behind and clean-up. A few hours later, I found myself lying on the floor in excruciating, paralyzing pain; it was like nothing I had experienced before. I was able to pull my body down the hall with my arms and get to the phone. The ambulance came and took me into the city, where I learned that my appendix had burst. They needed to operate immediately, and I would have to be hospitalized for two weeks because I was completely septic and required daily IV antibiotics and monitoring.

I wish I could say that those two events were enough for me to wake-up and make changes to my life, but that would be a lie. I viewed the bleeding ulcer and the ruptured appendix as weaknesses, and I was truly upset with myself for not being stronger. My "Wonder Woman" identity would be shattered if I showed weakness, if I needed to cut back, or if I needed that dreaded word "help". I defaulted to *"I am fine"*, it was like listening to a familiar old record that just keeps playing over and over again.

I missed the funeral because I was in the hospital, but we planned a trip to go and spread the ashes at Mount Robson Provincial Park. As a result of my recent health events, we thought we would make a weekend out of it in the mountains - a little R & R for the first time in over four years. We spread the ashes then headed up to spend a night in this picturesque cabin by Jasper's Pyramid Lake. It was something out of a painting, with the mountains and their mirror image reflected in the crystal-clear turquoise lake below. The only sounds came from loons and the occasional bumping of the canoes in the boat house, knocking against each other in the water. It was the perfect place to finally relax and a take a full, conscious deep breath.

Oh, please let it be a heart attack.

As I attempted to rest, a sudden, intense pressure came around my chest. It felt like someone was squeezing my heart and lungs in a vice. My hands and feet went completely numb, and I found myself gasping for breath. My ears were ringing and heat flooded through me, instantly causing my whole body to sweat. *I must be having a heart attack,* I thought.

In the emergency room, I explained all the symptoms to the doctor who carried out several tests. Not long after, the doctor came into the room and said, "Good news! You are not having a heart attack." My feeling of relief was brief as he proceeded to ask me, "Do you have an anxiety disorder?" I could feel my back arch up and my defensive reply was swift: "I work *for* those with anxiety; I don't *have* anxiety!" He paused, gently grabbed my arm, and began to explain that what I had experienced was, in fact, a panic attack. He gave me a few Ativan in an envelope and recommended I see my family doctor. I left in disbelief. "Wonder Woman" does *not* have panic attacks.

I decided to ignore the event when I came home, but the next three weeks were a living hell. I started having panic attacks daily, for no reason. I could hold everything together at work, put on a show that I was fine, but then I would come home and all the physical symptoms would pour in and hit me all at once. I could not sleep, I had open wounds in my mouth from grinding my teeth, my hands and feet were always numb, and, in my chest, it felt like I was drowning all the time.

Emotionally, I felt weak. I could not admit to others that I could not handle everything. I was full of shame at what I was going through. The irony was not lost on me that as a mental health professional. I finally went to my family doctor where the solutions offered to me were several medications, surgery for the ulcer, and a strong recommendation to quit my job. I, of all people, know that medication can have its place and purpose, but I also have seen first-hand how medications and their side effects can imprison someone within their own body. Honestly, that scared me even more than the anxiety itself.

Determined to find another solution, I began looking for alternatives to anxiety management. All of my research pointed to the need for a massive lifestyle change. I created a program for myself that was built on three foundational pillars: nutrition, movement, and self-care. It took me about eight months to address my nutritional deficiencies, support my adrenals, and bring balance back to my body. Today, I no longer have panic attacks or struggle with anxiety, and I truly feel stronger and healthier that I ever have in my life.

I now had firsthand knowledge of the positive changes that nutrition and self-care could bring both physically and mentally. I wanted to learn more and I wanted to share this information with others. I made the decision to go back to school to obtain a diploma in Holistic Nutrition. I am now a Certified Holistic Nutritional Consultant and a Natural Nutrition Clinical Practitioner. Additionally, I am a Certified Corporate Wellness Specialist, a Natural Weight-Loss and Wellness Coach, and a Certified Raw Food Chef. I am passionate about helping people achieve a healthy lifestyle balance, even if they are super busy. I also use my 3-pillar system to support people who struggle with anxiety, mood disorders, and chronic stress.

I opened Rejoice Nutrition & Wellness shortly after graduating, and I found that my main clientele was mostly composed of busy women, moms; the ladies who do so much for everyone else but don't take time for themselves. Because I had experienced what they were going through and healed myself using the alternative practices that was recommending, I was able to make a significant difference in their journey towards sustainable health.

Since then, through Rejoice, I have worked with many women and men who have transformed their lives by incorporating simple lifestyle strategies into their existing routines using a collaborative, customized coaching approach that is accessible and affordable to all. The transformational health stories of those I work with have been such a gift, they are daily reminders that those three pillars - nutrition, movement, and self-care - are essential for curating our best life and rejoicing in the most vibrant body possible.

Affordability and accessibility of services were essential to the curation of my nutrition and wellness business because some of the changes I had been able to make in my life were not financially possible for all families. Those who suffer from mental health issues often struggle with maintaining employment and a steady income, which, in turn, can make it difficult for them to obtain nutritious, whole foods. Statistically, mental health diagnoses increase the risk of food insecurity. Conversely, being food insecure increases the risk of mental health diagnosis. It's a vicious cycle.

As a result, I began the volunteer wing of Rejoice Nutrition & Wellness. It allowed me to work with local community food projects. I started an annual food drive with the local food bank that collects healthier, non-perishable foods and monetary donations. I also joined several advisory boards that address health, nutrition, and agriculture policy at the provincial and federal levels. Additionally, to support a more inclusive, holistic health care system, I began offering discounts and payment plans on all of my services to low-income families.

Everything in my life felt like it was back on track. My body was healthy, I felt stronger than ever before. I no longer had anxiety, and my businesses and volunteer work were making massive, positive changes in the lives of others. However, peace was still a missing piece to my personal puzzle. Nutrition and movement strategies were really easy for me. But, the truth was that, although and I could, with ease, counsel my clients to incorporate self-care into their lives, I still had not fully bought into and mastered the self-care part of the process *for myself*.

Don't get me wrong, I had a self-care checklist and routine that was textbook beautiful: quiet time, morning and night-time rituals, factoring in activities that brought me joy. But, despite all of that, I still found myself engaged in old patterns of behavior I knew were not congruent with true self-care.

Telling Fear to Finally "Eff-Off"

I would catch myself adjusting my words, saying sorry for things that were not mine to own, doing things I felt I *should* do to make others happy versus what I *wanted* to do. Basically, I was constantly dimming *my* light to keep others comfortable around me. I was still afraid of confrontation, and of saying what I really felt, because deep down I was afraid people would leave. For years, I kept a wall around myself. I could give others everything I had without a second thought, but never felt I deserved to receive that kindness in return. No matter what I ate, how much I worked out, or how many self-care activities I built into my days, it wasn't enough. I knew that as long as fear lived in me and I held on to beliefs that did not support my wellness, there would be a piece of my wellness puzzle missing.

I knew where this feeling of not being deserving of love came from. I did not have to dig too deeply; it always lived there just under the surface. There was a truth I had always been afraid to go after. There was a call I could make to silence still unresolved questions I had wondered about as a child. Why had I been put up for adoption? Had I been unwanted? Was there something wrong with me?

After some research, I found contacts for my biological family. My original intention was to acquire health information for my kids. What I did not realize at the time was how much learning my adoption story would affect my ability to let go of many unhealthy beliefs, and how having answers to my "why" questions would impact my heart.

In a society that glorifies labels like "Wonder Woman" or "Boss Babe", fear is perceived as a weakness; it's that thing that makes us feel like we aren't enough. That's why we hide it. I certainly had.

I decided it was time to tell fear to "eff-off" and make the call. Obtaining the answers to those essential questions was the most heart-wrenching experience of my life, by far. At the same time, outside of my children, it has also been the greatest gift I have ever received.

We may not choose all the circumstances and events of our lives, but we can choose how we react to them, We can have the right mindset. When we acknowledge our beliefs, ideas, assumptions, and fears, we can take a good, hard look at them and decide whether they support our health and wellness goals or not. It is up to us to decide whether to keep them or let them go.

It is not about wearing rose-colored glasses or denying our feelings, it is about choosing to not allow fear-based thoughts to determine our destiny. Fear is a huge barrier when it comes to creating the healthy, happy, fulfilling life we so desire.

Who could you be? What dreams would be possible? What obstacles could you overcome if you freed up your energy and didn't waste it on doubt? What if you could live the life you desire?

When I'm coaching clients, the pillar of self-care in my programs is now so much more than just a collection of recommendations for meditation, night-time routines, and journaling. It now involves helping people to let go of what holds them back, and encouraging them to turn up their light brightly and rock being who they are, without fear or compromise.

The feedback from my clients is not only that they have transformed their body and mind but their entire life is healthier and happier. They tell me that they have never felt better in their own skin. *This* is the most rewarding work of my career.

More recently, I was loading groceries into the back of my jeep one morning when I heard my cell ring from inside the car. I hit accept and a voice I did not recognize came out over the speakers. The man said he was the Chief Editor of Avenue Magazine and was calling to inform me that I was this year's Top 40 under 40 in the city. I had won the Community Leader Award. The next few weeks were surreal, a whirlwind of photoshoots and interviews; I couldn't believe what was happening.

Before I knew it, I was standing back stage at the auditorium, listening to the MC tell my story and highlighting my career. As I listened to her and waited for my cue to walk on stage, replaying in my mind like a movie was that jab from my childhood: "You will need to take care of Joanna when she is older to make sure she does not live on the streets,". Standing there, I released that thought and a large grin spread across my face as I heard my name called. When I took the first step onto the stage, I left that final piece of doubt behind me. I am deserving of being celebrated, I am worthy of this recognition, and, most importantly, I am enough.

Lessons Learned:

1) Listen to Your Body: don't ignore the signs of extreme fatigue and stress. In today's fast paced world, we are encouraged to "tough it out" and turn a deaf ear to our body when it tells us to slow down. Bad idea. They'll be subtle at first, but heed the warnings and don't be afraid to slow down. It could save your life.

2) Remember Take Care of Yourself: as women, we are the "caretakers". We tend to put the happiness of others first, while our needs take a back seat. Believe me, the best way to help others is to also take care of yourself. Remember to take that break, do something for you, and get your needs met. Self-care is not selfish. Everyone will benefit when you are healthy and well.

3) You Deserve to be Celebrated: one of the most important lessons I have learned is that fear, trauma, and doubt can cause us to create false truths about ourselves. They become our reality and often do not serve us. Dare to challenge those false truths and be courageous enough to rewrite your story. Rejoice in all that you are.

Mindset Tips:

1) Ditch "Wonder Woman": don't be so hard on yourself! When you feel the need to meet the expectations of others, consider what you would tell yourself if you were someone else. Would you expect perfection? Or, would you tell yourself that you have done your best? Can you give yourself a break? You'll be amazed at how relieved you feel!

2) Live Your Truth: being yourself is essential for finding happiness. Only *you* can live *your life.* Remember, you are enough. Don't be afraid to be you and follow your own counsel.

3) Let Go of Fear: fear of the unknown is your subconscious trying to protect you, but fear is also what is holding you back, sapping your energy. Remember that risk is part of a full life. Let go of fear. You'll feel so much lighter, so much more energized. Don't let the fear of what *could* happen, make *nothing* happen.

Aha Moments and Self Reflection

Note your Thoughts

Kristen Dawson

Kristen Dawson is the founder and COE (chief of everything) at Kristen Dawson EQ.

She is passionate about helping women re-establish their reputations with themselves. Kristen loves to speak, coach, and write about how we can live full of life and integrity.

Personally, she has released over 120 pounds and has learned that confidence has very little to do with what is on the outside and everything to do with what's inside. Kristen has created her own method of developing confidence called The Confident Way: 7 Steps to Unshakable Core Confidence. This method is based on how she went from hopeless and helpless to filled with love and joy.

Professionally, she has gone from casual employee to sought after corporate trainer, traveling and speaking with more than 1000 people on everything from basic operations to human rights and leadership.

Recently, Kristen left her corporate job after twenty-seven years with the same company to focus exclusively on serving those who need to hear her unique message.

Connect with Kristen:

www.KristenDawson.com

https://www.facebook.com/theconfidencecoachwithkristen/

https://www.instagram.com/kbdawson/

Chapter 4

My Life by the Numbers

By Kristen Dawson

Have you ever been on a diet and tried to lose weight? Perhaps you thought, *If only I weighed what I did in my twenties, I would feel good about myself.* How do you feel now when you look in the mirror or at photos of yourself? These are issues I've dealt with all my life.

As I transitioned from child, to teenager, to adult, I was often the largest person in the room. I felt like I didn't fit in. Yet, through these years of challenge, I learned the secret of courage and bravery that eventually helped me do the hard job of speaking in front of large groups. My deepest desire to be loved and accepted pushed me to become a leader and achiever with the secret hope of gaining the approval of others.

This inner strength served me well. "Feel the fear and do it anyway." I did that long before I heard the motto.

Over the years, many friends, colleagues, and fellow volunteers commented on my confidence. "Kristen, you are so confident. I could never do that." "Kristen, you walked up there like there was nothing that could stop you."

What they didn't know was that it wasn't true—I was not confident. I put on confidence like a coat and wore it like a mask. I was seamless in its application as I took off the mask when I was alone and then quickly put it on when others were around. I already had one layer of protection—the thick layer of fat surrounding me. The coat of confidence was one more cover to ensure no one knew my real condition: weak, wounded, and starving for love.

The layers of self-protection began early. Mom said I got fat when I was four. "Before that, you were normal."

Being larger than my classmates was cemented in my mind when I was five years old and a 'friend' called from the bottom of the slide, "Hey, *fatso*." I remember trying to come up with a witty, equally stinging retort. "Oh yeah? Well, you're a… you're a *skinso*."

Many details of my childhood escape me. I do recall the constant thought, *I am too big*. It came from doctors, family, and then finally from myself. I lived my life embarrassed and ashamed of myself.

At seven years old, I was enrolled in a gymnastics program. I loved gymnastics. My favorite move was the round off because I thought I did it quite well. It's a cartwheel where your feet come together in the air and then land together on the ground. In the middle of the lineup, waiting for my turn to somersault down the blue mats, I had to pee. I was too embarrassed to ask to use the bathroom. Instead, I peed in the middle of the gym floor, leaving a puddle of urine for someone to clean up. I didn't tell anyone. I hoped no one would notice as I tumbled down the mat, leaving a wet streak.

No one spoke with me about what happened. The leaders either were in shock or gracious enough not to bring it up. I think about the word *gracious*. Was it gracious for the leaders not to mention it to me? Was it gracious for them not to ask, "Are you okay?" As that seven-year-old, it was gracious just to move on. As an adult, I see an opportunity to demonstrate grace by engaging with the little girl who peed her pants. "Are you okay? Is there anything wrong? Let's get you cleaned up."

Despite being active in gymnastics and other activities, my weight continued to be an issue. Finding clothes that fit me properly was difficult. I was too wide and too short for normal-size clothes. It was the age of ten when the number on the scale became, to the exclusion of everything else, the focus of my life. It was then I tracked my life by the scale.

Ten years old: 95 pounds.

According to the doctor, I should weigh 95 pounds at age thirteen. His advice? "Don't gain any weight for three years, and you will be fine."

Twelve years old: 150 pounds.

I confessed this number to a friend in the dark shadows of a church hallway. She looked at me blankly. "So?"

Inside I was screaming, *So, that makes me a horrible person.* Outwardly, I was dumbfounded she didn't think my weight was a concern. This was the first time I remember being accepted, despite my weight.

I saw my first nutritionist. It was the first time I had a meal plan to aid in weight loss. I'm sure the piece of paper outlining one egg with one piece of toast for breakfast was probably put on the fridge. For me, it was a reminder of how bad I was because I wasn't able to follow the simple plan. It was my judgment in black and white, condemning me for every bite I wasn't allowed to eat.

Thirteen years old: 180 pounds.

Not only did I not stay the same weight for three years, but I doubled it. This was eighth grade. I went from large to uncomfortably large. From overweight to obese. I stopped growing up and continued to grow out. The change in weight was so rapid that I didn't recognize myself in the school photo. The girl with such a rounded face and chest wasn't me.

Twenty-six years old: 275 pounds.

I continued with the life I knew. Experts in obesity say it is a progressive disease. My *dis-ease* continued, and I continued to get bigger. Honestly, I didn't know why I had so much extra fat. Of course, I knew I ate too much food. But I didn't think I ate *that* much.

I wasn't sedentary and didn't let my size stop me from being as active as possible. I walked an hour to and from work a couple of times a week. I often explored the mountain paths with friends.

When I began to work as a letter carrier, I walked twenty kilometers (twelve miles) every day while carrying satchels full of mail. I still didn't lose weight. I knew I wasn't eating the calories that a four-hour workout session would burn. I didn't understand it. But what I did understand was that I was wrong, bad, and a failure for not controlling myself.

My mind's constant refrain was, *What's the answer to getting rid of this weight?* I counted calories and points; weighed and measured my food. I got injections. I paid thousands of dollars for countless diet and exercise programs. In the end, food was more powerful than my ability to control it.

I went to Overeaters Anonymous. It follows the exact same program as Alcoholics Anonymous but substitutes the word *food* for *alcohol*. I loved it there. It made so much sense. I had no power over food. I had to release my control. I found people who understood the constant battle within myself. It was the same as alcohol, except not.

You can survive without alcohol, but you can't survive without food. When your drug of choice is a life necessity, how can you live in sobriety?

My addiction felt like the devil and an angel were sitting on my shoulders. The angel would say, "Kristen, don't eat that. You've had enough." Or "You said you would only have one, and this is number four. It's time to stop." The devil, confident in my behavior, didn't say anything. I kept my hands moving until the food was in my mouth. As I chewed the food, I would say, "Too late now. I've already eaten it. So there."

Thirty-six years old: 320 pounds.

I had just delivered my third baby. I hadn't gained much weight for this pregnancy, but the fifteen extra pounds didn't come off. (You think it might have been the two cups of thick, sweet whipping cream I ate most days?) Despite feeling the heaviness of the extra weight, I attempted to approach each day with a positive attitude. When you have three kids within five years, life is often chaotic and filled with shouts of "Mommy."

It's embarrassing to say this, but I was usually the one throwing the temper tantrums—not the toddler. I wanted to be a good mom, but I was struggling. I wanted to be joyful and happy with my husband and children. The truth is, I was anything but joyful. The stress, anxiety, and depression of day-to-day life overwhelmed me. Food was the only way I knew to calm myself. I didn't want to be consumed with thinking about food. Yet, thoughts about the next time I could be left alone to eat in peace were never far.

I often escaped to the basement with my whipping cream and chocolate bars. Eating a container of ice cream while binge-watching TV was common.

The summer of 2009, I watched a show about people going through gastric bypass surgery. As I watched, I decided surgery was my answer. After years of feeling hopeless about losing weight and feeling *normal,* I believed it could be my way out. Finally, a light at the end of this miserable tunnel.

I began researching, asking around. People had heard about the surgery. There were surgeons who performed this life-saving physical procedure. As a Canadian, our healthcare system allows access to health care without many out-of-pocket expenses for general care. I had to make the costlier decision to self-pay for the surgery. In my mind, there were two options: 1) Stay a hopeless woman, growing larger each day, navigating the emotional pain and physical restrictions of obesity; or 2) Pay $22,000 for the surgery—which would make *everything* better.

This decision was easy. No contest. "For everything else, there is MasterCard."

From the time I contacted the clinic, flew for my pre-op, and had the surgery, it was less than two months.

Thirty-seven years old, November 2009: 320 pounds

Thirty-seven years old, May 2010 (six months later): 200 pounds.

I felt amazing. I began to run from place to place. Someone asked me, "Why do you do that?" I said, "Because I can." My appearance was commented on continually, and I noticed more people making eye contact. My smile grew, as it was now more prominent on my face, and more people smiled at me.

An unexpected change happened. For years I carried a thick layer of fat and was used to people going through the door in *front* of me. One day, someone not only held the door for me to grab it behind them, but also waited for me to walk through *first.* I was caught off guard. People usually didn't do that. The change made me feel respected.

How do you feel when you see someone who has obesity? How do you act around them? Prior to surgery, I was classified as Super Morbidly Obese Class III with a Body Mass Index of 54. (The normal range is between 20 and 25.) As a woman with morbid obesity, I always knew that people treated me differently. They weren't bad, or mean, or intentionally ignorant people. Well …some of them were. Most were just ordinary people at the store, the mall, and walking on the street.

Thirty-eight years old, March, 2011: 169 pounds.

The last time I saw this number on the scales I was twelve years old. I only maintained it for one day. The next day, was up to 170 pounds.

Forty years old: 195 pounds.

I often asked myself, "Why do I keep gaining weight? Why can't I stop eating at just one? Why is my home life still filled with stress and strife? Weren't all these problems supposed to stop when I lost weight?" I was thoroughly convinced losing weight would fix my life.

Forty-one years old: 205 pounds.

In the middle of the binging and internal pressure of never feeling good enough, I held onto a kernel of truth—there was *more* for me. This belief kept me busy, running down the different paths I thought would get me to *more*. Even though losing weight didn't fix my life in the way I expected it to, it offered me the possibility of actually accomplishing more. Maybe it was the change in how others saw me and treated me differently. Maybe it was the increased energy and physical abilities I experienced after losing 150 pounds. Maybe.

I started thinking about what else I could do. The possibilities of moving up the corporate ladder. About living the life of influence

I had always craved. I took courses, applied for promotions, and worked part-time jobs to expand my life.

Crash.

The winter holiday season was busy. There were parties, family get-togethers, and shopping. I was also working overtime at my job. My first day off, the symptoms of depression hit. Getting out of bed was a monumental effort. On the drive to see the latest Disney movie with my husband and children, I cried all the way to the theater. All I wanted to do was die. At one point I thought about opening the car door and jumping out in the middle of the freeway.

We went to the movie *Frozen*. It captured so many of the emotions I felt. The songs swirled in my mind. *Let it go. Don't hold it back anymore. The good girl is gone. Let it go.*

Let me go.

The feelings of hopelessness, extreme exhaustion, sadness, and the constant tears were not new. I was diagnosed with major depression over two decades prior. I had experienced multiple depressive episodes where I thought death was the best way out.

This experience felt different. It was deeper and stronger than previous episodes. The depressive thoughts were more powerful and invasive than I felt before. People may think living for family or for children, is motivation to stay alive. My problem was I believed my family would be much better off without me. If I were gone, at least my kids would have peace…finally.

In retrospect, it would have been best for me to go to the hospital, but I didn't know it was an option at the time. The emotional pain was unbearable. Accessing a psychiatrist was not possible because there were not enough doctors to meet the demand. The call I received from the mental health worker is vivid in my mind. "Will you kill yourself today? No? Good. We'll see you for your appointment in five months."

During this time, I ate, slept, saw my psychologist, and worked. My husband continued to manage the family. I managed my emotions with food. With a combination of time, medication, and therapy, I emerged from the darkness and resided in a fog of functional.

Forty-three years old: 230 pounds.

There was no way I went through surgery, and all of this effort, to go back to the old me. My first thought was, *There is a problem with my hormones or body. How else could I get back up to 230 pounds?* I was eating more vegetables. I couldn't eat big meals or a lot of sugary foods because of how the surgery changed my body. Too much food was not the problem. I saw an endocrinologist, but, the tests revealed nothing. I was sure *that* was wrong.

Out of desperation, I went to a nutritionist. They hadn't been very helpful in the past, and I certainly didn't think I would learn anything new.

This time was different. This nutritionist seemed more informed and encouraging. I learned at least one important lesson: eating Lindt truffles every day adds up to a lot of calories. I honestly hadn't realized exactly how many I was eating until she suggested I start tracking my food.

I began to look at my food intake differently. I hadn't eaten a lot of food or been ill by eating too many sweets at one time. I learned that for my body and level of activity, I was simply eating too much.

Win.

How was knowing I ate too much a win? There was no judgment. There was no shame. I wasn't *bad* for eating more than my body needed. It was just a fact. If I didn't want to continue to gain weight, I could choose to do something about it. Also, if I didn't want to do something about my weight, I could make that choice. There was freedom in not beating myself up. I stopped the endless criticisms and verbal punches, and now there was the mental space to do the work.

I started incorporating some of the ideas from the nutritionist. I paid more attention to what I ate. Food lost some of its power. In reality, I wonder if food lost some of its power, or did I start finding mine?

As I started finding my power, I decided to leave my fifteen-year marriage. I use the word *decided* loosely. I debated the idea endlessly in my mind. I told my husband that I was thinking about divorce. After what felt like an eternity, a few days later he said, "It's alright for you to go."

Can you imagine that? I wanted to leave but still needed him to give his consent. My husband didn't have an issue. *I* did. He wasn't demanding or controlling; it wasn't a requirement of the relationship that he give me permission. I needed his approval. If he said it was okay, then I was okay.

Forty-four years old: 215 pounds.

I moved into my friend's spare room. There was no question that the kids would stay with my husband. He had provided them with stability in the years that I wasn't able. He had been the primary parent since they were small.

My mental health was better than two years earlier, but I was experiencing more mental illness than mental health. After reading *The Depression Cure* by Stephen Ilardi, I started a checklist for increasing my brain health:

- Read ten minutes. Check.
- Go outside. Check.
- Take vitamins. Check.
- Exercise. Check.
- Journal. Check.

Self-care was my goal. My checklist wasn't perfect, but I made efforts to follow through. I realized that I was willing to exercise for my mental health but not my physical health. It took thirty minutes of very fast walking to feel my brain start to brighten and my mood begin to lighten. My days were filled with work and self-care. I googled what others did for self-care. Not much of it seemed as intense as my regimen. One post said, 'I read for fifteen minutes before I pick up my kids from school. That's my *me* time.' Others talked about going to the spa or a five-minute break from the kids.

I mentioned to my psychologist that I was doing two full hours of daily intentional self-care, and these people were reading in their car. Her comment was, "Some people need more care than others." How true.

I needed two hours every day, in the beginning. My heart and soul were battered and bruised by childhood, addiction, society, criticism, judgment, and shame. The wounds were deep, and the recovery period would take time.

Forty-five years old: 205 pounds.

I never imagined this life of freedom. When I began to take care of myself, to truly give my inner self what I genuinely needed, I flourished. I started making the food choices that my body needed, rather than what I wanted. I craved the physical activity that gave my body an emotional release. Now my body knew what it felt like to be cared for. And I liked it.

Forty-six years old:??? pounds.

I haven't stepped on a scale in over a year because numbers no longer matter to me. If I had to guess what I weigh, I would say between 196-200 pounds. I know I am smaller because everyone likes to tell me I've lost weight, and I buy clothes that are smaller in size.

My confidence has exploded. I've learned that confidence is knowing I have done what I believe is right. I have faith in myself and my abilities. I am always going to do my best, and my best is all I can do. Finally, confidence is trust. I have built the trust in myself that I will not judge or be harsh. I have given myself the gift of following through on my promises. I trust myself with my heart and my dreams.

As I write this, I have really stepped out with faith. I resigned from my job of twenty-seven years to speak and coach full time. I believe in my desire to help others learn how to trust themselves. I want to let women know there is so much mental and emotional freedom available to them. They are much stronger than they believe and already have everything they need.

What do you believe about yourself? Do you believe in your own abilities? Do you trust yourself with your dreams? I know beyond a shadow of a doubt that you can do everything you want to do. And if you need to, you can borrow my faith in you until you can uncover your own.

Lessons Learned:

1) The things we think and believe about ourselves is what determines how we feel, not how others treat us. People will respond to you based on their perceptions of what they see and feel.

2) The food we eat and the number on the scale isn't about will-power. Eating isn't about 'right' and 'wrong'. It's about the grace and love and compassion we give ourselves.

3) Demonstrating to yourself that you are trustworthy is crucial. You are always there to see and hear everything that you say and do. The only one to ever convince is yourself.

4) It is possible to be thankful for the obstacles, and when that happens, they truly become opportunities.

Mindset Tips:

1) Talk to yourself. Do you have the wise voice in your head? That is your true self. Allow it to give you the care and nurturing you need.

2) Remove the judgment from your actions. When you mess up, and you will, tell yourself it's okay. You are not 'bad'. You did something that wasn't in line with what you said you wanted. Without condemnation, it is much easier to make the changes we desire.

3) Ask yourself what you are willing to do. If you say you want to eat healthier, and find yourself not doing it, be honest with yourself. If there is a part of you that is not ready to do it, that's okay. Honor that part and ask it what is going on.

Aha Moments and Self Reflection

Note your Thoughts

Clinton Harris

Clinton Harris is a personal development expert, life coach, entrepreneur, trainer, motivational speaker, and author. He has worked with many well-respected experts in his field. Working in organizational leadership, educational institutions, with families and the military, he has served to help people all over the world for over a decade. Clinton hails from Chicago, Illinois but has since worked in a multitude of cities and foreign countries. He also has years of experience in family counseling, drug, and alcohol addiction counseling, smoking cessation and suicide prevention.

Clinton has served in the United States military and since exiting earned multiple degrees in the fields of IT and business. Clinton will soon release two solo books, *Shenandoah Dreams* and *Honed By Fire*.

Connect with Clinton:

www.clintonharriscoaching.com

https://www.facebook.com/ClintonHarrisCoaching/

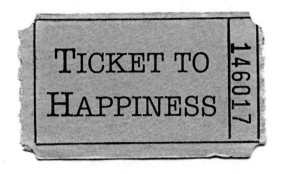

TICKET TO HAPPINESS 146017

Chapter 5

Life's Un-Punched Ticket

By Clinton Harris

Inner-city Chicago would have been a challenging place to grow up anyway, but when fate or circumstance added a tumultuous home life to the mix, it was a recipe for disaster with downright catastrophic results. I used to sometimes analyze my situation and find a way to make it comical in some way. I would look at my life and think that it was as if someone had taken a lot of stress, a little hell, and some danger to create a devastating practical joke, that wasn't really very funny at all. Having to brave the streets of the South Side with the simple purpose of living, going to school, and growing up without being shot is one thing, but making it home only to be threatened with mortal wounds by a family member is a whole other can of worms. In my world, there was no such thing as a safe place.

I grew up on a fairly nice, residential street, only half a block from the beach. We were not poor and didn't want for much as a family, at least materially. My father had a good job and a good partner in my mother but there were other, more important wants that I felt every minute of every single day. From the outside, we appeared to be living the proverbial "American Dream" but the truth was that we weren't living the dream, or living at all. We were just alive and surviving, barely.

The truth is that I grew up in an abusive household where sexual, psychological, and physical abuse were by various relatives. My sister ran away when I was five and my brother when I was six; he is now serving a life sentence in the state penitentiary for his transgressions. My mother finally left when I was seven, leaving me at the mercy of what went on in that house.

I never knew what to expect. Would I be left alone, or would I be assaulted in some way. From the time I was seven years old until well into my teenage years, I slept with a knife under my pillow, in a futile attempt to feel safe. But there was no such thing as safety in my world.

Curiously, I was never actually beaten but I did suffer innumerable indignities, acts of violence, and humiliation. Garbage cans were emptied on me while I slept if I forgot or failed to take out the trash. Dirty dishwater was poured on me if I forgot a single spoon, knife, or fork in the water. When I lost my keys as a child, I had to wait outside until someone finally decided to let me in. Fingernails would be dug into my skin, drawing blood and reaching the white flesh beneath. My door would be kicked in and I would be threatened with death about once a week. On multiple occasions, a handgun was placed against my head, chest, and in my mouth. Sometimes I would be locked n the basement for a weekend at a time, in the dark, with only one can of food. I was constantly cussed out, called names, and put down.

This is the first time that I have attempted to tell my story, and this isn't the half of it, but you get the picture.

My home life was a freak show that no one in their right mind would ever want any part of. As if that wasn't traumatizing enough, I also had to contend with the violent environment outside my home.

I lived on the South Side of Chicago. Unless you've been living under a rock, you are aware of Chicago's reputation as one of the most violent cities in the country. The South Side, in particular, is a breeding ground for violent crime, drugs, prostitution, and, most notably, it's high murder rate.

Over two summers in the '90s, more than three-quarters of my friends and acquaintances were wiped out. After a while I no longer had tears to cry. I don't know if I became more mentally tough with each occurrence or if I simply grew numb to the pain, whatever it was, it became my new normal.

What is certain, my situation was not conducive to success. It was more like a perfect storm for breeding a monster. For my entire childhood and into young adulthood, I was swimming in a sea of dysfunction.

To summarize, I had no immediate family support, I had little to no contact with my extended family; the home I lived in was an unsafe, even dangerous, environment where I was subjected to the most horrific abuse, and my mother was out of the picture. My neighborhood literally had an unquenchable appetite for human life and there were few, if any, community resources available to incentivize and facilitate change.

When I put it that way, doesn't it sound like a cornucopia of happiness? I'm kidding, of course, but humor was how I coped at the time, and in some ways still is.

I would find ways to go somewhere else in my mind. I ordered every travel magazine available, reading them all multiple times. If I couldn't physically move my body, I could at least transport my mind elsewhere. In my early years, I played sports almost from the moment I got home from school till I had to be in the house, but that particular avenue of escape disappeared as the neighborhood violence got worse.

As the years went by, I felt more and more defeated. Although I had I always excelled in school as a young boy, by the time I reached high school, it was no longer the case. I just didn't give a solid damn anymore.

I attended classes and turned in nothing. I was just there, and that did nothing but push me further down my depressive spiral. By the second quarter of my freshman year, I had straight F's. Not because I couldn't do the work, but because I was no longer allowed access to school facilities. My father, somehow, was not my legal guardian; and, without a legal guardian, I couldn't attend class. My daily routine was reduced to spending my days sitting in the school auditorium until the situation could be sorted out. It never was.

By the end of the third quarter, I was told not come back until I had a guardian. I sat there at home, watching some of my friends graduate, earn their diplomas, and begin their lives. It hurt. Peering outside from the stairs where I sat inside my house, I felt nothing but pain. I asked myself, "Why am I here? What is my purpose? It seems that I only exist to be a punching bag for life itself." I couldn't graduate and my life was taking me nowhere. I hit rock bottom and sank into depression. I was lost. Lost, that is, until one day everything changed.

My "awakening" happened overnight.

One day, I simply decided that I would not allow the defeatist mindset I had developed to hold me captive any longer. I was going to prove to myself what I had known as a child but somehow had forgotten as I aged: I was not a loser or a failure. Change was going to happen because I decided that change didn't have a choice. I decided if change was not going to volunteer itself, then change was going to be "voluntold."

At the age of seventeen, I woke up one summer day and I decided to complete my GED (General Education Diploma). That day, I went to the nearest center for adult education and signed up for classes that started on the following Monday.

Within one hour on the first day of class, the instructor said, "Get out of here and never come back. You don't belong here!" I was caught so off-guard, I didn't know what to think or say. I didn't understand why he wanted me to leave or why he was being so harsh. All I had done was literally answer every question he asked. Now he was telling me to leave.

He followed me out and said, "Son, do you understand why I threw you out the way I did?" I shook my head, no. "I have never engaged with a student, or anyone for that matter, that has known all of the answers. You do. Yet, I can tell that you also don't believe in yourself." That man, whose name for the life of me I can't remember, did so much more for me in that moment than I had done for myself in years. He restored my faith in myself.

From that point on, I was unstoppable. Yes, I had a few setbacks, but now I had the determination to work through the challenges and strive for success no matter what. I signed up to take the GED test on the very same day that instructor kicked me out and I passed with flying colors on the first try. I had reached a crossroads. I was on the threshold of adulthood and I could choose my own path. I was finally in a position to create my life as I chose, to follow the dreams seeded by those travel magazines and books I had read so many years ago; I wasted no time in doing it.

First, I joined the military where I received valuable training, reinforcing natural character traits that would later support my desire to help others on a large scale. I became a Hospital Corpsman in the U.S. Navy. It hadn't been my first choice, nor even my last, but I was nudged in that direction by my superiors and I am grateful for it today. I came to understand what being a corpsman truly meant. I learned what that caduceus medical symbol stood for and I was proud to wear it.

Later, I became an EMT (Emergency Medical Technician) and earned certifications in Surgical Technology, Smoking Cessation Counseling, and Drug and Alcohol Addiction Counseling. Although I had never endured the pain of addiction myself, I had witnessed firsthand the devastation wrought by addiction in our household while I was growing up. I not only found that I liked the medical field, I was good at it. But that wasn't the end of my ride.

After leaving the military, I went back to school and earned my Associate of Arts in Information Technology, my Bachelor's in Business Management, and my MBA. But school wasn't my endgame; it was the beginning of my path to success.

I became a school counselor, school manager, and a National Director of Military Education and Partnerships.

Eventually, I decided to go back into healthcare but this time on the business side. As a business coach, I helped people understand how to effectively open their own elderly care locations.

I found that I really enjoyed coaching and I started to work for a Brendon Burchard company where, until recently, I helped individuals to be more productive and happy. I guided them toward the light in their life, even if initially they couldn't see it themselves. Working with Brendon, I came to realize that I also had a profound message to share. Not only was I encouraged by the feedback I got from my clients, but I had a passion to share my message burning within me. That fire was the pilot light for something great.

I became a life coach, privately coaching individuals to become better versions of themselves. The authenticity and empathy I brought to my work were a source of comfort for my clients, who said that they found our work together refreshing, revitalizing, and very helpful. I began to write a book.

I am now a motivational speaker, guest speaker, and will soon be hosting my own yearly personal development seminar(s), masterminds, and coaching events.

As a youth, I never saw myself as a motivational anything, much less a role model. I never imagined that I would be speaking at seminars, coaching people, or writing books. I just wanted to survive my neighborhood and, more importantly, my home life. But, something inside drove me to go out and help as many people as possible, regardless of their circumstances or mine.

We all face adversity in life; it's how we respond that defines us. We always have a choice, even if we can't see it at first. Our options are not always going to result in a win but that doesn't mean we should give up. Losing is not the test, perseverance is. Never stop trying, and you will be fine. The most important principle is to learn from your mistakes so you can avoid repeating them. As human beings our mind can be our greatest asset, as long as we take the time to nurture it and keep it focused on our goals.

My main objective in telling my story is to impress upon you that it doesn't matter who you are, where you come from, or what you have. What matters is what you want, what you strive for, and what action you take to achieve your goals. We all have a mind, but we must choose to keep it focused on the positive because, unless we train it to stay focused on "yes, I can" we run the risk of getting stuck in "no, I can't."

Life truly is what we make it; a lesson I learned after many years of believing that I had to accept my fate and would go through life without any hope of ever achieving success. I thought that my ticket to happiness would be left un-punched forever. I was wrong. Once I changed my mindset, I came to understand just how completely wrong I had been.

No one is destined to fail, nor is anyone destined to succeed. Our outcomes are the products of our choices. My choices and determination are what got me to where I am now. No, I can't and won't say it will be easy for you, because it's not. What I can say is that setting goals, doing what it takes to reach them, and succeeding, will be one of the most rewarding and enriching journeys you will ever embark on.

Education and experience were how I chose to deliver life's un-punched ticket to the conductor. What I found when I got there was that the conductor for my life had always been me. I also discovered that what I had learned on my path to success and happiness was not meant to benefit only me. It was also meant for a larger stage, where I could use my passion and energy to benefit others.

If my story has taught you anything, I hope it is that you are your own conductor in life. It is up to you to grow and thrive. Don't allow yourself to exist another day with your ticket to happiness left un-punched in your pocket. Punch your own ticket and outperform your past. Choose to focus on positive goals, do what it takes to achieve them, and then set your sights on a new challenge. Aim for the highest peaks and climb the mountains you have yet to conquer.

Lessons Learned:

1) Your Past Does Not Equal Your Present: nobody would have bet a penny on my success based on my history, and yet I was able to overcome everything I went through. It is never too late; don't let your past define you. You can start now, wherever you are in life, and create a better, brighter future.

2) Educate Yourself: I think you'll agree that unless I had decided that, no matter what, I would acquire the skills I needed to get out of my situation, I would never have made so much out of my life. Once you know what you want, go get whatever education and skills you need to make it happen. If I did it, you can do it too. I know it!

3) Keep Your Eye on The Prize: remember, it doesn't matter who you are, where you come from, or what you have. What does matter is that you stay focused on the prize, on your goal, on what you want; whatever obstacles you encounter along the way. Resilience is the key. If you have that, success will be yours.

Mindset Tips

1) A Positive Proactive Outlook Will Really Change Your World: it sounds cliché, I know, but positivity and a desire to make something out of my life despite my circumstances are what allowed me to succeed. Don't let anyone or anything bring you down for more than a second. Your outlook will determine your future.

2) It's Not a Fail If You Learn from Your Losses: as I mentioned above, the issue is not whether you win every time but whether you *learn* every time. Treat your losses and failures as life lessons and you only will grow stronger and wiser; you will reap the rewards in the end.

3) Choose to Succeed: Success is, first and foremost, a state of mind. You have to decide to win, choose to succeed. Be a winner in your mind first and the rest will follow.

Aha Moments and Self Reflection

Note your Thoughts

Kristin Herr

Born and raised in Tupelo, MS, Kristin Herr knew at a young age she wanted to explore different parts of the world while living life to the fullest.

Kristin studied marketing at the University of Southern MS but had a calling to become a Cosmetologist because she loved making people feel good. She left college behind to pursue her passion and moved to Mandeville, LA to study Cosmetology.

After graduation, Kristin moved to Santa Cruz, CA where she landed a job managing an Aveda Concept Salon.

Kristin has been on a journey of self-transformation and self-love. In this process she found her true calling as an entrepreneur. She now has a professional coaching practice helping women overcome limiting beliefs so that they can take their careers to the next level and live the life they were destined to.

She now lives in Truckee, CA in the Sierra Mountains with her husband and two-year-old son.

Connect with Kristin:

https://www.facebook.com/kristin.brown.3950

website: www.kristinherr.com

Email: kristinherr@kristinherr.com

Chapter 6

You Are Meant for More – Don't Settle

By Kristin Herr

Have you ever had a defining moment in your life when you asked yourself "How did I get here?" I sure have, and it really got me to thinking.

One of my very first memories, as a young child, is of my Grandmother criticizing me for being chubby. I wasn't what I'd call fat, but I was about 10 lbs. overweight.

I remember visiting her clothing store with my parents, one time, and she embarrassed me in front of some customers. I don't remember what was said exactly but I do remember being really upset. When we left, I cried. My parents got into an argument because my Mom was mad that my Dad wouldn't confront his mother about this issue.

This was just one of many memories that really stuck with me. What you must realize is that this went on for years. I remember it starting as early as five years old and continuing until I was a young teenager. I never felt like I measured up, or was thin or pretty enough. My Grandmother would tell me how much better

I'd look if I were 10lbs lighter and that clothes make a person. Looking back now, from an adult's perspective, I think she honestly believed that she was helping me, not realizing the damage her words and criticism would do to a young girl who just wanted to feel loved and be accepted by her own Grandmother.

Today, I know that the poor relationship decisions I later made in life can be traced back to these early experiences, when I felt not good enough and began to form a core belief of unworthiness.

When I was in high school, I was in a serious relationship with a guy I ended up marrying. I did love him, but I came to realize that I used him as a way to run away from everything: my family, the strict Southern Baptist rules I was grew up with, and the guilt and shame of having had pre-marital sex.

In a lot of ways, we grew up together, but he never fully matured. After eight years of marriage, I was done and wanted out.

Here's the thing, though: you can leave a marriage and even try to run away from your own issues, but, at the end of the day, they will still be there.

When I left the marriage, I was happy and excited about my life, but I wasn't alone. I had met someone who gave me the attention I craved, and we were having a lot of fun. However, I had jumped into another relationship too soon.

We lived over 200 miles apart but made an effort to see each other almost every weekend. It sounds good, but, as it turns out, though, it wasn't the best way for me to really get to know him.

Not that there weren't warning signs. I chose to ignore them. I was naïve and looking for love in all the wrong places. Yes, I was a living cliché. That was me. Spot on.

I decided to move in with this man who took me 200 miles away from a job and close friends that I loved. I even gave up an amazing opportunity to buy out one of the partners at the high-end salon where I worked. I thought this was love.

Remember those warning signs I told you about? Well, a reliable source called to tell me of an incident that had occurred between him and one of his parents. The caller wanted me to know about the incident before I made the move. It didn't change anything, though.

Initially, things were okay. It wasn't all rainbows and butterflies, but it wasn't awful. I found a job but had to take a huge pay cut. Nevertheless, my boyfriend expected me to pay rent on the house he owned and was already living in before I was ever in the picture. I did.

To be honest, as I write this, my heart is racing. How had I even considered making this move? Geez!

The first time he lost it, I'd been living with him for a couple of months. I remember him screaming and calling me every name in the book, pushing me, and then punching the pictures on the dresser of my mom and dad when they were younger. The pictures broke and his knuckles were bleeding; I was shocked.

I tried fighting back when he pushed me. I learned right then and there never to do that again because it only made things worse. He threw me to the ground. I was crying and begging him to stop. He was out of control.

Once things quieted down and I was being obedient to stay safe, he came to me crying and saying how sorry he was. I now know this is textbook behavior for abusive people. They twist your words and somehow make you feel sorry for them. This is how the cycle began. It went on for two years. He would flip like a switch, usually over nothing. He'd go crazy and lose control.

I remember one night when he got really angry. He put a pillow over my face. I was crying and screaming for him to stop. This is the only time I honestly thought he might kill me. I had a busted lip and a bruised eye and couldn't go to work the next day because of how I looked.

I wish I could tell you that this was the turning point for me. That this was when I said enough is enough but no, not even close. The cycle continued. Through the tears he'd say he was sorry and he loved me. Then life would calm down for a little while until something else set him off.

I remember him sitting at the table one day, eating the breakfast I'd just made for him. All of a sudden, he flipped his lid and was screaming at the top of his lungs, right in my face, telling me how worthless I was, that I made him do this to me, and that it was my fault.

There were times when he would tell me that I was crazy to think he was abusing and mistreating me and that, if I really felt that way, I should leave.

Manipulation at its finest.

There were many incidents like these. I stayed. It's a vicious cycle. Abusive relationships go like this: uncontrollable anger and abuse; the abuser cries, says how sorry he is, and that it won't happen again; things are good for a little while, and then it all begins again.

I did love his family, though.

His parents loved their son deeply but had struggled with his anger issues. They did everything they could to help him; offering both financial and emotional support. But, as they discovered, you can't help someone who doesn't think they have a problem and blames everything on someone else.

Still, I stayed. And, on top of everything else, I racked up a ton of credit card debt in the process. I would pay for things I couldn't afford, to keep him "stable"— remember, I had taken a huge pay cut and had to pay him rent.

So, what happened? What made me change?

Well, I went to a baseball game. You must be thinking, "What are you talking about? Are you crazy?" Nope. A simple San Francisco Giants baseball game with a couple of good friends: my former employer, Julie, and a former coworker. I told them I wasn't happy and wanted to move back to Santa Cruz.

Julie said she wasn't happy with her current manager, so we started talking. She offered me my old job back. My sweet former coworker offered me a place to live; she was going through a divorce and could rent me a room. And so, the plan began.

Change takes time. Nothing happened immediately after the ballgame. A few months went by before I started to get my ducks in a row. I told the boyfriend that I was probably moving back to Santa Cruz and taking my old job back to pay off my debt. I didn't tell him I was ending the relationship and, truth be told, I still wasn't one hundred percent sure what I was going to do.

By the time Thanksgiving and Christmas came around, I had committed to my employer. The plan was to move at the beginning of the year, but I was scared and wavered. You might be wondering, "How could that even be possible?" Well, being in a toxic relationship is a very twisted thing.

I visited my family for the holidays, and I remember the ride back to the Memphis airport in my parents' car. I was flying back to California. I had told my parents I was thinking of leaving my boyfriend. I was in the back seat and my mom asked me if I'd made a decision. I told her I had not, although I had already committed to Julie.

My parents dropped me off at the airport and I could feel the anxiety building. I hopped on the airplane and made it to Denver where I had a layover. I was pacing and struggling emotionally.

It might be difficult to understand how someone who is in an abusive relationship, and has an opportunity to get the hell out, can actually be thinking of staying. The only way I can explain it is that I was beaten down. I doubted myself beyond belief and in, some twisted way, loved him. I also thought that he loved me and that, just maybe, we could still make it work.

I called Julie from the Denver airport. I told her I was having second thoughts and freaking out. I remember it like it was yesterday, her words to me were, "You don't have a choice. I already fired my manager." All I can say is thank *God* she didn't give me a choice. I was in a weak moment and I needed someone to lay it out for me.

When I got back to California, I started packing. I rented a moving truck generously paid for by my employer, and I got ready to leave. It was the beginning of January and freezing cold outside. On the day I was going to pick up the truck, things escalated. He got violent and angry. He threw my stuff out on the lawn and me along with it. Soaking wet hair and all. He also threw my phone because I was trying to call the police.

I was able to gather the up the pieces and put my phone back together enough to call my girlfriend. I called my sister, in tears. I was a mess. When my boyfriend threw me down outside, I fell on the concrete, injuring my wrist. I was also freezing out there waiting for my friend to come to the rescue. Thankfully she arrived soon and talked some sense into my boyfriend. We left to pick up the moving truck and buy a brace for my wrist.

The cycle continued. He cried and apologized. I stayed the night with him. Seriously, what was wrong with me? The next day I left. I drove that U-Haul by myself to Santa Cruz, while my friend followed behind in my car.

I got settled in and started my job. I'd love to tell you I was doing amazing and that life was great but that would be a lie. I was broken. I didn't know how to pick up the pieces.

So, I started therapy and went to a support group for battered women. Both were of some help, but I wasn't doing amazing at my job. I was doing okay, but not like before. The lack of self-esteem and confidence were taking their toll on my job performance and impacting most areas of my life. I was sad and I didn't know how to be alone.

I spent a lot of time with my close friends and avoided being by myself. I rarely spoke with the ex for the first few months but then, for some reason, we started talking again. I even saw him when I went back to his town to visit my dear friend. Why did I do that, you ask? I really don't know. He was handsome, a smooth talker, and a master manipulator. He pulled at my emotions and heart strings. We started speaking more often and even saw each other a couple of times.

Fast forward to May of that year when I met my future husband. I had sworn off men after moving back to Santa Cruz. I didn't want or need a relationship, and, although it was hard at first, I was perfectly happy being alone. It was better than going through another terrible relationship.

My now husband lived in Oakland, California at the time. We had mutual friends who had tried to get us to meet for several months. Neither one of us had any desire to meet the other. Then, my friends tricked me. They said *The Dead* were playing and asked if I wanted to go. I agreed. On the way there they told me Sean would be there. I didn't think too much about it, honestly. We met and he was nice but it definitely wasn't love at first sight. I had a great time at the concert and got to experience *The Dead* for the first time. Although Jerry Garcia had died by then, I enjoyed hearing remaining members play.

We all went our separate ways after the concert, and I didn't hear from Sean for a couple of months. During this time, I was still meeting the ex-boyfriend from time to time. Crazy, I know.

When Sean and I finally did start dating, I knew he was different. He was respectful, fun to be around, and genuinely caring. What is more, everyone seemed to like him, and no one ever said anything negative about him. Most importantly, I could be honest with him, which was something I really needed at the time. I told him some of what I'd been through and explained that, as a result, I was holding back part of myself. I was still gun-shy. He didn't mind. He was a sounding board who was very mature and emotionally stable. He was a great listener. He heard the good, the bad, and the ugly, and accepted me as I was. He let me work through my emotions.

Finally, almost a year after I left him, I told the ex-boyfriend I was done. I'll never forget that moment. I was at home in the bathroom, using the toilet as a chair with the lid down. I was on the phone with my ex-boyfriend. He was crying and so was I. I told him it was over and that I hoped he treated the next person he was with way better than he had treated me. I hung up the phone. That was the last time I ever spoke to him. It was freeing and I knew I was where I was supposed to be and with whom.

I was finally free of the ex-boyfriend, but I wasn't free of my demons.

Time went on and I moved in with Sean. He was in Oakland and I was in Santa Cruz. When he first asked me to move in, I told him I had been there and done that already, and it hadn't work out for me. Being the person he is, his response was, "I think it will be great and you can just use me." Like, who says that?

I eventually did make the move but, first, I continued with therapy and the support group. I was afraid of making the wrong decision again and was worried that I had a lot of baggage. But, in the end, moving in with Sean was great. We never argued, almost to a point of fault. Before I moved in with him, I actually I picked a fight with him just to see how he would react.

I enjoyed living in the Bay area and working in Berkeley, but we both knew in our hearts that we would probably want to get married and start a family. We also knew that doing so in Oakland wasn't very appealing. We decided to move to Truckee, which is in the Sierra Mountains in the Tahoe National Forrest, just a short 25-minute drive to Lake Tahoe.

We got married in Thailand two years later and decided to start a family. At this time, I wasn't really working on my self-development. I was having fun and enjoying life with my husband. We traveled, went to concerts, had nice dinners out, and we supported one another.

I got pregnant two months after we started trying. We were excited and so scared. Then, a few weeks later, I started cramping and bleeding. We lost the pregnancy. It was heartbreaking but we waited a few months and then started trying again. It didn't take me long to get pregnant. I had a good feeling about this one and thought for sure everything would work out.

I lost the second pregnancy in July of 2014. Talk about heartbreak. The doubts start creeping in. What's wrong with me and my body? I went to the doctor, but they didn't want to do any tests unless I had a third miscarriage. Apparently, miscarriages are way more common than I realized.

That fall, my mom got diagnosed with terminal cancer, my husband's grandmother died, and I had to put my dog down. My heart was broken. I remember looking my husband in the eye and telling him I didn't know how much more heartache I could take.

That Christmas, we went to visit my family in Mississippi. It was my mom's favorite holiday. She always made it so special for us and I wanted to be there with her for one last Christmas memory. My gut told me she wouldn't be alive next year.

On New Year's Eve my husband and I went to New Orleans. On our drive back home to Mississippi, I lost another pregnancy. I didn't cry; I had expected it. The hardest part was that I knew my mom's time was limited and I wanted her at least to know that I was pregnant when she died. It didn't happen.

My mom died on Halloween, 2015.

My husband and I were waiting to start trying for a baby again. I was getting more tests done. I was emotionally fragile, and I couldn't bear the thought of another miscarriage. Then something miraculous happened.

On April 1st, 2016— exactly 6 years to the day after I moved in with Sean —I found out I was pregnant again. I was a few days late and I just had a gut feeling. I remember it very clearly. I was headed to post knee surgery physical therapy and I told my husband that I thought I was pregnant. I told him I took an ovulation test because I had one laying around and it showed a smiley face which means you are ovulating. It detects the same hormone that the pregnancy test detects. I also told him, "Don't get your hopes up."

I took another test, which confirmed that I was, indeed, pregnant.

The pregnancy was viable this time and I wanted to be the best mother possible. So, I started more therapy to work through the baggage. Just because I was in a happy marriage and finally having a baby, didn't mean I had overcome my limiting beliefs and self-doubts.

On December 5th, 2016, at 8:36 AM, I held my healthy baby boy in my arms for the first time, and my life was forever changed. The love I felt for this child was immeasurable. Didn't he deserve the *best* mom possible? A mom who could love herself and show up for herself and her family? Of course he did.

I knew that I had to change. I had to change my thoughts and my self-limiting beliefs. I had to do it fast. I'd been through so much and I was finally a mom.

Here's what you need to know. Change is not easy, but it is worth it.

I was tired from lack of sleep and I was still grieving the loss of my mom, but I had to do something once and for all to be done with this *unworthiness* nonsense. Do you know I actually thought my son might not love me or accept me because I wasn't a skinny mom? Who thinks like that? *Me*, that's who.

How did I change? I used every ounce of spare time to read about personal development, listen to podcasts on mindset, meditate, and write in a gratitude journal. I started thinking about how I could be the person I was meant to be.

I also made changes at work; I took a leap of faith and changed companies. I needed a way to work from home online, so I could make money while staying home with my son. I couldn't stand the idea of working away from home five days a week and putting my son in daycare. Not after everything I went through to have him.

Now, I work two days a week at the Salon, doing hair, and get to be home with my son five days a week. It's a win-win because my husband stays home with our son the two days that I work.

At the same time, with all of the personal development doing, I started hearing my voice. I realized that I have a calling, that I'm meant for so much more, and that I have a story to tell. I also came to understand that I loved helping people. I loved inspiring them. I knew that I could use what I had learned in my own life to serve them.

I went out and got my life coaching certification. We all need a little coaching sometimes and it seemed like something I would really be good at. As a coach I could help my clients and hold them accountable to help take meaningful action. I wasn't going to be a therapist focused on the pain of the past. I was going to be a coach helping others get to where they wanted to be.

What do you want? What is stopping you from achieving it?

I have found that there are many people who, like me, want more out of life but don't believe in themselves. They don't believe it's possible for them even if they know deep down they are meant for more. I know that I can help them get moving forward.

I got into the hair business 18 years ago because I like helping people. I like making them feel good and I like connecting with them. Now I'm taking those skills to a new level. I've discovered my true calling and I know that I can have an even greater impact and help more people than ever before.

If there is just one thing you get from my story, I hope it is that you'll believe in yourself, no matter what. Know you are good enough and worthy. It doesn't matter what has happened to you, what you've done in the past, or how broken you may think you are; you are more than enough, and you are worthy of every dream you have.

If you are here, on this earth, you are here for a reason. God, the universe, whatever you want to call it, doesn't make mistakes, and it's no accident you are here. You are a miracle. Playing small and feeling sorry for yourself doesn't serve anyone. Go after your dreams, no matter what other people say. If there is something in your heart that you want to do, go for it.

Lessons Learned:

1) Your weight, looks, and past do not define who you are. You are a child of God and here for a reason.

2) Love, forgive, and be gentle with yourself. Speak to yourself like you would a best friend who is hurting: with compassion. Do the work to love yourself more than anyone else.

3) Go after your dreams and your heart's desires. If there is something on your mind and in your heart that you want to do, then do it. It's never too late. Don't wake up on your death bed and say, "I sure wish I'd done…" Instead, do it now, no matter how old you are or how crazy it may seem to others. You've got one life and it's up to you to live it.

Mindset Tips:

1) You have to work on your personal development and your thoughts daily. Do whatever it takes to change your beliefs. You can change your beliefs and your identity. Start acting as if you are the person you desire to become. It doesn't matter what has happened in the past or if you aren't where you want to be in life yet.

2) Write down and say your affirmations in the form of a "why" question. It's easier to get the mind answering *why,* than to try and change a statement part of you still believes is true. For example, instead of stating, "I love myself", ask, "*Why* do I love myself?" The brain can't help but answer. This is something I learned from Noah St. John. I recommend his book, *Afformations.*

3) Be *you,* be vulnerable, and don't be afraid, or ashamed, to share your story. We all have a story and you have the power to make a difference in other people's lives. Find your voice and speak up.

Aha Moments and Self Reflection

Note your Thoughts

Chris Koper

Chris grew up in Wisconsin, spending most of her childhood outdoors playing. Her father, who survived fighting in the Philippines during WW2, believed in fitness and instilled its importance in Chris at an early age.

Education had not been a priority, but she was encouraged to attend Dale Carnegie, where she learned to speak publicly and overcome her shyness.

Chris became a mother late in life and working from home enabled her to instil strong work ethics in her daughter. Lauren is now striving to compete in the Olympics as an alpine ski racer. Chris feels parenting was the biggest blessing and learning curve in her life.

After repeated adversities in life, Chris turned inward to see what she could change in herself to create a better life.

Chris is passionate about horticulture and garden design. She volunteers in her community and runs a blog that teaches people about the healing power of gardening

Connect with Chris online:

https://ckgardeningforlife.wordpress.com

http://www.facebook.com/CKgardenforlife

https://www.instagram.com/chris_helps

Chapter 7

It is Never Too Late to Find Your Passion

By Chris Koper

It all started with an awful breakup. It's one of the best things that could have happened to me since I obviously had not yet learned what kind of person was good for me. He was an adult child of an alcoholic parent and verbally mean and abusive. We were headed to Hawaii for a trip he earned selling mutual funds. The day before we were to leave, I found out that he was taking his lovely banker instead. I was working as a hairdresser, and he even tried to come in for a haircut before he left. My only regret was that I didn't oblige him and then slip and cut the front of his hair off! Alas, I am much too ethical.

To get over this heartbreak, I kept myself busy. One of my clients was a ski patroller at one of the hills in Wisconsin. I asked him if he would help me learn to ski better, and he said, "You bet." So off I went skiing one weekend. My client was very excited to tell me there was a ski patroller from Canada visiting, and he had helped set up the head patroller to work at the 1988 Olympics. So, he set me up to ski with this Canadian, and we really hit it off.

We kept in touch, visiting each other off and on, and after about a year, he asked me to move up to Canada. On one of my visits, we went to the immigration office where he sponsored me (paid a fee) and signed a document that he would be responsible for me financially for ten years, so I would not become a burden to the system, should I fall on tough times. There were many obstacles to overcome: checkups, interviews to make sure things were on the up and up, as well as tons of paperwork. Immigrating was a very time-consuming process. The stipulation was that we had to be married within ninety days of arriving. He and I agreed to all these rules. We decided we were spending the rest of our lives together, so we got engaged. Big mistake. Ninety days is *not* enough time to get to know someone.

I thought I had really thought this life-altering experience through and was so excited to start my new adventure. I guess I thought the grass was greener on the other side of the fence and a new location would make my life complete. I had not yet figured out that my happiness was dependent solely on myself. When immigration gave us the green light, I gave notice at work, packed up all my things and put them in storage, except for my clothes and a few personal items. I said goodbye to my family and off I drove to Calgary. I drove the 1526-mile (23 hours, 11 minutes approximately) trip in two days. As I arrived on 16th Avenue late at night, I could see the bright lights of Calgary on the horizon. I had never seen anything like the big beautiful 'WELCOME TO CALGARY' sign that greeted me. What a feeling in my heart, arriving to this wonderful city.

It was days before Christmas 1988, and we drove with his sister and brother in law to Yorkton, Saskatchewan for the holidays. I met his parents for the first time, and I had bought him some coal candy (black liquorice) for his stocking. This made him upset as he thought I was implying he was naughty. **Strike one.**

For New Year's Eve, we were at Fortress Mountain. Driving to the mountains was breathtaking, and I was absolutely mesmerized by the beauty. Yes, that is a long time ago as Fortress is no longer open. He had started ignoring me at his parents, and by New Year's the situation was unbearable for me. **Strike two.**

I had had a hairdressing job lined up before I arrived, but it takes time to build a client base, and I had not picked a busy enough salon to start. He thought I was not making enough money, and wanted me to become a secretary to his ex-wife. Then I found out he had moved out of their house and taken everything with him while she was away visiting her parents. I thought he was crazy, and my answer was an emphatic, "NO." **Strike three.**

I was exactly thirty years old – ready to grow up and start a family. I had no idea I would be thrown back into the party scene all over again. That is not to say I didn't have some fun. I remember going out to a bar on 11th Avenue. He did not want to go home and change, but as we were sitting there waiting for friends, one of his female buddies came along and said, "Let's go change." He left me there and went with her. Do you see a pattern emerging here? **Strike four**.

While I sat there alone, a random young man walked up and asked if I was by myself. At the time I was, so I said yes. He put his Bible on my table and went to get a drink. Just then, a female friend of mine showed up and I was no longer alone. Thank God…she moved the Bible to someone else's table, and I got some company I knew. I was too shy to tell this person I was expecting company because I didn't know when. I was happy when my friend was bold enough to remedy my situation.

When my fiancé arrived back with his friend, we started our night. This would happen often. His friend (who worked in corporate), asked me to lunch after that night. I was excited to start new relationships, but she blindsided me by telling me not to come between their friendship. I was flabbergasted and speechless.

We also went on a skiing trip with all his friends; driving by bus with a bunch of happy people drinking paralysers (something I had never heard of) and blueberry teas. One of his friends had a slip of the tongue as they got tipsy and said my fiancé went to the French Maid several times a week for lunch. For those who don't know, the French Maid is a strip joint with '*incredibly* good food'– or so he said. I also found out that none of his friends knew we were engaged. Seriously? **Strikes five and six.**

After many episodes of being caught unawares, I tried to talk to him about our problems. I thought I should move back home. He said he wanted to keep trying, because if he couldn't make it with me, he couldn't make it with anyone. Blindsided yet again. What was wrong with me for putting up with such BS?

As the ninety days came to an end, he could not bring himself to marry me. But since he had signed a document, he had to accompany me to the immigration office to say why he changed his mind. The immigration officer told us if we didn't get married, I would be deported. Then came the tears and the knot in the pit of my stomach. The immigration officer kindly told me when they issue a deportation, you don't have to leave that minute. You have some time. I couldn't believe my ears. Deported? I was American, white and from the same continent. I didn't think of myself as an immigrant.

His brother-in-law took me to lunch to feel out my intentions. They were worried I would hold him financially responsible for me till I got it all together. Lucky him that I didn't ask for a penny. His other sister and brother-in-law had a meeting with me to say goodbye and inform me that they were appalled at his behavior – that he had, in fact, been married several times. He had broken up with each wife in the most vindictive ways, and I could not believe how blind I had been. I was so devastated.

I left and moved in with one of his ski patrol buddies who was separated. But not before checking with his wife to make sure she was OK with the situation. I did not want to get in the middle of any more problems. The only support network I had access to was *his* support network. Think about that. I found a new job at a larger salon and got busy fast, because I was experienced. I worked hard and met wonderful people in the Silver Springs and Scenic Acres area.

During this time, I gathered documentation to see if I could stay in Calgary. It would have been expensive to move back home and start all over again; not to mention I was *so embarrassed*. My clients became many, very loyal right off the bat and wrote letters to immigration as to why I was an asset to Canada. I gathered newspapers showing there were so many hairdressing job openings, so I could prove I was not taking opportunities away from Canadian citizens.

When the time came to go back to immigration, the owners sent their dad with me for support. I can't tell you what that meant to me. I was scared, nervous, emotional, and the immigration officer asked me what made me so good that people would write about me in such a positive way. I said through my tears, "You will just have to come in and find out for yourself." The day came when I got word that I had received Landed Immigrant status. I was ECSTATIC. I became part of my wonderful hairdressing family. Some time after I was official, my immigration officer's hairdresser moved to Europe, and since he lived in my area, he came to me to get a haircut. I did not recognize him because he was out of context. I cut his hair several times before I recognized him. He laughed and said, "I was wondering how long it would take you." I cut his hair for years afterwards. I still have clients to this day that have been coming to me for thirty years.

In the meantime, living with this ski patroller became unbearable. I kept the house clean and made meals for his dinner parties while *he* took the credit. Once, his wife brought her vacuum over and told me to get busy. It was absurd, since the only one cleaning in the first place was me. When his wife would walk in, he would hug me or get close to me because he could see it made her jealous. So that was it for me, and I moved in with a friend.

During this time with my friend, we would pour over cookbooks together and plan meals for our dates. We had a caricature drawn of our prospective dates and had them picked up by a white limousine one night. It was then that my ex wanted to try to get back together. My heart wanted it so badly, but my brain did not allow me to get past the hurt he had previously caused.

I had to get used to the differences between Canadian and American culture. What are they, you ask? For starters, here are some word differences: Canadians say 'roof', Americans say 'ruff'. Dollar is pronounced differently. Some Canadians say 'hey' a lot after some sentences; Canadians withdraw money from the bank with a check, Americans with a check. Canadians wear runners; not tennis shoes or sneakers. You book off work to go on holiday in Canada, and you go on vacation in the US. When I first moved here, I wanted to 'grill out' some steaks. My fiancé turned the oven on. When I walked out with a plate of raw meat intending to put them on the BBQ, it was not on. When I asked for a rum and soda, I got rum and seltzer. And WTH was poutine? I had a craving now and then for a gyro and couldn't find any, till years later when I found out a donair was the same thing. I had never heard of a hat being called a toque, a hoodie or gaunch. Again, WTH? Zee and Zed? About and Aboot? In the US you might ask to use the bathroom, not the washroom, and when asking where the water fountain is, I might ask for a bubbler. We also don't say sorry as much.

I had done some backpacking through Europe in my early twenties. In England and Italy, I had a couple of episodes of rude behavior. I never knew why until I moved to Canada and found out most Europeans don't love Americans (even though I was clean and neat, with money to pay for things, and was always respectful). One of the other things I found different about being American was if someone skipped in front of me in a line-up (queue), I would be inclined to tell them to get to the back. Canadians, I found, would be upset and say nothing. I observed Canadians to be generally more up on world issues and found myself more interested in politics. One more thing: Americans tend to tell it like it is, and I found Canadians quieter, letting you know in a more roundabout way of their displeasure.

Then I became a Canadian citizen, which made for dual citizenship. It was emotional, empowering, and it was in my new home that I found my greatest passion.

My husband used to have a landscape company and had a beautiful yard. When I moved in, I asked if I could put a tomato plant in his garden and he agreed. It only had one tomato which I cared for and fondled every day till I broke it off! The fruit was small, but I wrapped it gently in newspaper and stuck it in the cupboard. I checked every day to see if it had ripened. One day I reached in expecting a small tomato and found a huge one. My husband had replaced my little tiny one with a big juicy red and ripened tomato, much to my surprise.

Four years later, my daughter was born. I stayed home to raise her and dabbled in hairdressing, but I needed something more – for me. So, I signed up at the Calgary Zoo for the Master Gardener course with friends, and that went on all winter. Once finished, I realized I liked gardening and took Landscape Design 1 and 2.

My daughter started at the preschool at our West Hillhurst Community Association. I helped raise money, and the preschool paid for the plant material to redo the front garden. That was my first garden project.

After that, my daughter was taking skating lessons at our community center and her skating coach had become the manager of the facility. When she found out I had taken landscape design, she asked me if I would design a community garden for the center because it was becoming popular. It took me a year to think about it, but I finally said yes. First thing I did was contact our liaison from City of Calgary Parks for instruction and restrictions.

I thought I would do a design, get my husband to build it since he had owned a landscape company, and that would be that. NOOOOO, not even close. I had to fill out paperwork from the city to get a $5,000 in-kind grant, and they were very sticky and methodical. Thank God, because it forced me to be organized.

I formed a group of community members to help, came up with several budgets, wrote grants, planned and got donations and discounts on the materials. It was a much bigger project than I had ever imagined. I had never done a budget in my life; it was a huge learning curve. I contacted the Calgary Horticultural Society, and they gave me two people from the Community Garden Resource Network for extra support and guidance.

I then solicited community members who were builders and asked that they become foremen for our building day. We had a day where my husband and I showed the guys the prototype and how we wanted it built. They got so excited that they built the first layer of the gardens that day.

The gardens were honeycomb shaped because the manager did not want them to look like coffins. The design was great because it stayed clean and neat looking as everything was lined up perfectly. One volunteer had become a close friend and his help was invaluable. He has since moved to a different part of Calgary, and I like to think that he was inspired by our work together on that garden because he now runs one himself and we collaborate often.

I made an effort to meet many of the people at the Horticulture Society, the city, and other community gardens. I volunteer at the Calgary Garden Show every year now, meeting thousands of gardeners from all over the country. Once the gardens got up and running, I wrote grants, and we put on gardening classes every year. We became one of the top gardens in Calgary and were on the Calgary Horticulture Garden Tour one summer. We were slowly becoming a hub for other gardeners to come and learn. People from the City of Calgary Parks and other community gardens began recommending me for new garden build guidance. I really enjoyed this role but sometimes I was disappointed when people were unwilling to put in extra time and effort to achieve goals unless they were getting paid. If you want to get to the top, you do whatever it takes, convenient or not.

It was during this process that I realized that I am good at garden design and community gardening life. My self-confidence grew, and I was making all kinds of connections. However, I had family give me grief for volunteering so much, but it was fulfilling me and making me feel whole. We started helping people with and without disabilities to volunteer in our garden in a capacity that worked for them and made them *feel good* (It is key to find what works for the volunteers to ensure they are fulfilled and happy.)

People and management changed at Community Associations and working there became difficult, so I took the summer off. My daughter was in middle school at the time, and the principal asked me to help work with the kids in the Spanish program to help them design their decrepit courtyard. I gave a class in design to the 6th-grade class (my daughter's grade). They then formed groups and had to go measure and create designs of their own.

The teachers picked the top two or three designs in each class, and the groups had to present to our panel. I could not just pick one design, so I took as many of the interesting concepts the kids had and did many concept drawings incorporating their ideas, so many kids felt they had contributed.

After one concept was picked by the principal, we started trying to put together budgets, getting approval from the Calgary Board of Education, getting donations and writing grants. My husband and I did a stepping stone class with the kids. Some stones were sold to raise money and then some were incorporated into the courtyard. The kids were so pumped, and it was a little feather in my cap (heart) to have the kids recognize me and come up to talk to me when they would see me out and about.

A grant was written for Coop Community Spaces, and we received approx. $80,000. I wrote a grant for the National Bank (One for the Youth), and we were awarded $5,000. The pathways were made of bricks that the families of the school could pay to have their child's name, family name or sayings engraved upon. The politics were very tough, and once I had most of the details together, one of the parents stepped in, took over and kicked me out. The principal went along with it, and that crushed me. I couldn't figure out why they didn't just say, "You did so much, let someone else have a turn." Instead, it was like being on the Apprentice show where Donald Trump points his finger and fires everybody. I hung in there like glue so that the project continued to uphold the kid's ideas as much as possible. In the end, the courtyard was completed. I got recognition and the kids got their space. Tt appeared on a TV commercial (you can find it on YouTube by typing in Coop Community Spaces 2015 - Senator Patrick Burns School Project). Another big learning curve and growth experience.

Politics happen from time to time in everything you do. I was having trouble dealing with stress when bad things happened for stupid reasons. It took me almost sixty years to realize I had to have a good look inside myself. What do I do that causes these negative things to happen? Why did my channel always seem to be on replay constantly?

It was at that time that my girlfriend from Wisconsin sent me *The Secret* DVD. I totally believe that your thoughts can put ideas in motion. I had the wonderful opportunity to meet Dr. John Di Martini, who talks about how the brain works and how the energy of the universe converts to motion by the power of thoughts and words. I made the decision to become a more positive person and stop being a victim. I try not to dwell on negative things anymore, although I do catch myself sometimes and must self-correct.

I have come a long way, and I have helped many people redo their yards. I have more knowledge under my belt and a lot more confidence to follow my dreams and live a better life. I found my passion (gardening and design) and plan to pursue more knowledge in this area as well as in *every* area of my life. I want to be better at everything: my marriage, being a mother, making money, cooking, photography, organizing, being happy and fulfilled while being open to learning. I want to pursue speaking more (thank goodness one of my past bosses sent me to Dale Carnegie when I was young, shy, and made me be a manager).

I feel more confident than I ever have in all my life. As I am reading about other people overcoming obstacles and adversity, it humbles me, and I am grateful for all I have. I find joy in helping others, and I choose to smile.

Lessons learned:

1) It is never too late to find your passion and pursue it. I can attest to this statement.

2) Take an honest look inside yourself to see what keeps repeating itself and why. Only then can you see what needs changing.

3) It is not selfish to stick to your guns about what makes you happy. Only *you* can make *you* happy. Stop waiting and blaming others for your unhappiness. Others will love you more if you love yourself.

Mindset Tips:

1) The friend I met and worked with during the building of the community gardens taught me not to do things that are not enjoyable or fun. Life is too short.

2) You will know you have found your passion when you don't mind all the hard work. You won't feel as tired.

3) It is hard work climbing to the top and making things happen. Hang in there and persevere, I would not have gotten to stay in Canada and achieve all I have by quitting and feeling sorry for myself.

Aha Moments and Self Reflection

Note your Thoughts

Aditi Loveridge

Aditi Loveridge is a certified life coach and mindfulness meditation teacher. She is also the owner of Pregnancy Loss Healing and a non-profit organization called the Pregnancy & Infant Loss Support Centre, located in Calgary, Canada. Aditi helps mothers who have experienced pregnancy and infant loss to reconnect with trust (and love) so that they can step beyond anxiety and fear. Her work includes supporting mothers who have recently experienced loss, are trying to conceive after loss of any kind (pregnancy/infant loss, failed IVF, missed adoption), are pregnant again after loss, and those still struggling after the birth of their baby.

Before working as a certified coach, Aditi had a successful career as a social worker in women's sexual health. She now draws on her social work, mindfulness and coaching skills to help mothers connect with their present moment experiences so that they can engage wholeheartedly in their lives.

Connect with Aditi:

www.pregnancylosshealing.com

www.facebook.com/pregnancylosshealing

www.instagram.com/pregnancylosshealing

Chapter 8

Rooting Back to Love After Loss

By Aditi Loveridge

I was whisked down the hallway, leaving the light and the warmth of that room behind. The back of the cold, dark, and sterile ambulance a deep contrast.

This would be the beginning of my journey into motherhood. Rooted in fear. Rooted in distrust. Rooted in uncertainty.

Three years earlier I had landed back in my hometown of Calgary. It was eerily quiet compared to the hustle and bustle of the streets in Toronto that I had grown accustomed to. As I looked around at the empty spaces around me, I reminded myself that this was 'temporary'. Moving back to my hometown was a decision I had made because I wanted to go back to school. I had left the salon I owned back in Toronto in hopes of growing a career as a social worker. To save money, I found myself back in Calgary, living with my parents at twenty-seven years old. "This is only temporary" had become my mantra as I begrudgingly settled into my new life in an old space.

My ten years in Toronto had distanced me from many of my old friends in Calgary. So, upon my return, I began hanging out with my cousin and his circle of friends. I became quite close with these people, spending every weekend together. These new-found friends really helped my 'temporary' move back to Calgary feel like…home.

Larry was one of those people. I will never forget the night I met him. For years, I had heard about my cousin's roommate, Crazy Larry. I had heard about this goofy man that stayed up all night playing video games naked. When my parent's doorbell rang that night, I opened the door to find a rather handsome (fully clothed) man with a case of beer casually swung over his shoulder. This man standing in front of me looked so kind, friendly, and fun. Not what I had expected.

Over the following few months, Larry and I would party together and were often the last two standing after all the other guests had left. One particular night at the end of a party, Larry and I kissed. Or as he would tell, I kissed him.

That kiss filled the empty spaces that I didn't realize were in my heart, and at that moment, the empty spaces of Calgary ceased to matter; the quiet welcome. I knew then that my life was not going to be the same.

One month after that kiss, Larry asked me to marry him in true Larry fashion. After a night of playing the video game *Rock Band* at a friend's house, Larry and I were in my car outside chatting about how in our short time of dating, our souls had met. At one point Larry said, "I just love you so much I want to marry you. Will you marry me?" Never in my life had I ever been so sure of anything. So in my car on that quiet street, my heart and soul said yes. Larry jumped out of the car, took off his shirt (in -15-degree weather) and ran a shirtless victory lap. He didn't have a ring. He didn't get down on one knee. He showed up just as he was ...completely unexpected, clothed in nothing but love.

We married eight months later in an intimate ceremony that blended both my Indian and his Canadian roots.

Like any other newly married couple, people began to ask Larry and me *the question*. They didn't want to know how married life was going or where we were spending Christmas that year. No, it was *the question.*

The question that is always brought up as a topic for small talk, but it is never a small topic: When are you having kids?

Those words always made my heart beat a bit heavier in my chest, because the truth was, I wasn't entirely sure I ever wanted kids. Though Larry said he wouldn't mind having children, I was still unsure.

I was a newly-wed woman with a promising career as a social worker. After years of feeling lost, I had finally begun to connect with myself and feel comfortable in my own skin. My confidence as a woman was only just starting to sprout, and I was afraid that having a child would bury me. I always thought that having a child meant choosing between an inner love and an external one. I did not know at the time that I could hold both loves simultaneously.

Then we got our dog, Zion. Growing up, I never had a pet. I had no idea of the deep bond that a human can develop with a furry little being. He brought me so much joy and a sense of purpose that I never felt before. The love I had for him didn't feel external. It was more of an extension of the love I already had within.

I found myself thinking that if I could love a fur baby so much, imagine what it would be like to have a human one. I also began to see that creating a life with Larry didn't necessarily mean taking away from the life we had built together…perhaps it would enhance that life. Just like Zion had.

A few weeks later, I took the first step in building a family; I stopped taking birth control pills. Larry and I didn't have any expectations and didn't want to put too much pressure on ourselves. I wasn't tracking ovulation or any other process. We simply made a choice to become rooted in love and possibility.

When I got my period soon after, I wasn't sad or shaken. I took it as a welcome sign that my body was ready to conceive in due time. I did notice, however, that my period was different. It was shorter in length and much more painful than before. So painful that I had to take half a day off work, which hadn't happened since I was a teenager. I chalked it up to my body regulating herself after years of being on synthetic hormones.

At the time, it was December, and I was invited to a holiday party at my friend's new apartment. I was having a great time and looking around with so much joy. *How lucky am I?* I thought. *I have a wonderful husband, a great job, great family and friends. I have found my place.*

Then in the washroom, I saw blood. It wasn't a lot, just minor spotting. But it was enough to shake me; leaving me feeling completely ungrounded.

I woke up the next morning feeling off. I had a mild radiating pain in my stomach, my head was hurting, and I was still spotting. This was normal for a day after a party, right? Regardless, I called into work sick and spent the day in bed with a hot water bottle and Tylenol.

By that evening, the pain had gotten worse, not better. I was still unsure of what was going on. I thought that maybe I had the flu.

The next morning the pain and the spotting had both increased.

I can picture the emergency room I was taken into as vividly as the day I entered. It didn't look like a typical hospital room; it felt warm and inviting. The bed was against a wall of windows that let in the brightest morning sun.

That day, the nurses did some routine tests, including a pregnancy test. A few minutes, later the nurse casually walked in and said, "You are pregnant. But you might be losing it."

All I heard in the warmth of that room was "you are pregnant." The "you might be losing it" was a denial so deep that my heart refused to connect to the words.

I'm pregnant. I'm pregnant. I'm pregnant.

I sat in disbelief.

The doctor walked in and said she needed to do an internal exam. My mind was spinning—I was going to be a mother. The reality of life growing inside of me dissolved any of my earlier apprehensions about having a child. Though we had not set any expectations, at that moment, the walls came down, and I became a mother. I felt so deeply rooted in love.

I winced as the doctor pushed on the left side of my uterus, asking if I felt pain.

With care and sympathy, the doctor said, "I am sorry, but I think you might have an ectopic pregnancy." I learned that this occurs when an embryo grows in the fallopian tube instead of the uterus and is life-threatening for the mother.

Before I could ask any questions, a team of medical staff that entered the room and I was being transferred by ambulance to another hospital with better imaging equipment.

I was whisked down the hallway leaving the light and the warmth of that room behind; the back of the cold, dark and sterile ambulance a deep contrast.

This would be the beginning of my journey into motherhood. Rooted in fear. Rooted in distrust. Rooted in uncertainty.

No longer rooted in love.

The doctor at the second hospital didn't think it was an ectopic pregnancy and wanted to send me home.

I quickly realized that I was much further along in my pregnancy then what he thought. I figured out that the 'period' I had earlier was not a real period. It was an, in fact, another telltale sign of an ectopic pregnancy.

But that doctor refused to listen to me.

That doctor saw my brown skin and labeled me. He mocked me by speaking in an Indian accent (which I do not have—I was raised in Canada) when he thought I couldn't hear. He refused to see me. He dismissed me and sent me home.

From that point, it was weeks of tests, more bleeding, more pain, more ignorance, and more attachment. I became very attached to the little life inside of me struggling to find its way.

Ten days later, I was brought back into the emergency room, death settling into my skin. It was indeed an ectopic pregnancy. My growing baby was pushing on my fallopian tube, causing it to rupture. A tragic contradiction of life and death.

On December 26, 2011, my first baby and my first experience of motherhood were taken from me. I woke up from surgery and my baby—the one who was desperately fighting to grow inside me, the one who had become an intimate part of me—was gone; with nothing more than a scar on my abdomen as evidence that my baby had ever existed.

In the darkness of the night, as a new year crept in, and I allowed myself to cry for it all.

In the months that followed I continued to navigate grief while also trying to conceive again. My loss had highlighted that though there was uncertainty about having children earlier, I wanted nothing more than to hold a baby in my arms.

I found out I was pregnant for a second time, and what should have been happy news brought a feeling of worry, stress, and anxiety. Instead of focusing on the life that had been created, all I could focus in was what could be taken from me. I was completely rooted in fear.

No longer rooted in love.

An ultrasound helped Larry, and I relax a little when we saw the baby was growing where it should be. Looking at the image on the screen, I let go of the breath that I had been holding in, slowly allowing myself to imagine our future with a child.

As the days and weeks rolled on, I found myself connecting to the possibilities that this pregnancy brought. I would fall asleep each night cradling the barely visible swell of my abdomen in both of my hands—allowing myself to dream of this growing life.

And then I woke up one morning and I didn't feel pregnant. The connection to the growing life ceased to exist. Something was wrong.

An ultrasound that morning confirmed my worst thoughts—our baby had stopped growing.

"I am sorry, but there is no heartbeat."

I am not even sure who said those words. I just know that they cut through my heart like a sharp knife. And with the "no heartbeat," I felt mine shatter.

As I lay on the cold, dark, and sterile ultrasound table, the doctors told me my 'options'. I could have a D & C (Dilation and Curettage) or go home and allow my body to let go of the baby on its own. After having my first baby surgically removed, I chose to go home and let 'nature' take its course.

Five weeks later, my body and my heart had still not let go.

Five weeks is an extremely long time to carry both life and death inside you simultaneously. Those days and weeks were some of the hardest of my life. I decided to quit my job because they did not support my choice to wait. I had no other plans for work or for my future.

All I knew was that I had to let my body do its thing. I knew in the depths of my soul that this was imperative to my healing.

Then one late night I sat in meditation (meditating had become the only way I knew how to reconcile this ambivalent space I had found myself in), and something happened. In the silence of the night, I got a deep message: *Sometimes you have to lose everything in order to regain yourself.*

That message cut through the darkness and touched my soul. It was as if daybreak had come—the light of that message filled up the empty space in my heart, and I felt my body…surrender. I felt my heart, body, and mind connect.

Root back to love.

I allowed the tears to come. I felt the tension in my body and heart lessen. I must have sat there in surrender for an hour before I felt like I could find the strength to pick myself up off the floor and crawl into bed.

The next morning, I started bleeding. My body and my heart were finally ready to let go.

In the ensuite bathroom, surrounded by loved ones, my body let go of our second baby.

In the immediate days that followed, I was overwhelmed with gratitude. It might sound strange to feel gratitude for a labor that didn't result in a living baby, but the experience restored faith in my body and in myself.

Sometimes you have to lose everything in order to regain yourself.

Two months later, I found myself pregnant for the third time. This time was different. I felt more love and trust in my body. Fearful thoughts would creep in, but I would remind myself that this was a new pregnancy. A new moment.

Fourteen weeks into that pregnancy I woke up for work and found my underwear covered in bright red blood. I let out a wail so loud and heartbreaking that I didn't even recognize that the sound came from me. I called Larry right away and asked him to come home. On the way to the hospital, through tears, I told him, "If we lose this one, I am done". And I meant it; my heart couldn't take this anymore.

After what seemed like hours, we were finally sent in for an ultrasound. I found myself once again lying on the familiar bed—cold and in the dark. The ultrasound tech had a student with her, and I thought, *Great, today is the day she learns about death.* As they probed my body, there was silence.

I was taken back to another room and told to wait.

Twenty minutes turned into an hour. An hour into two. Finally, the doctor came in and said, "Congrats. You have a healthy fourteen-week fetus." They did not know what had caused the bleeding but said that everything looked normal and they sent us home.

Larry was smiling from ear to ear the entire car ride home. I smiled back, but inside I felt the tug I knew all too well. The tug back into fear. The tug back into darkness. The blood had jolted me out of safety, and out of love. I couldn't see past the flag of death that was waving in front of my face.

From that point forward I struggled deeply with fear. I woke up every morning and obsessively checked for blood. I started to disconnect from my baby. From my body. From love.

When we finally made it to the twenty-two-week ultrasound, I was a ball of nerves. We walked into the 'gender' ultrasound expecting to leave with the happy news of whether we were having a boy or a girl. Instead, we walked out finding out we were having a girl...that had a high likelihood of a developmental condition.

As I lay on the cold, dark, and sterile ultrasound table once again, the doctors told me my 'options'. I could have an amniocentesis, which came with a risk of miscarriage. I could wait until I deliver to find out, or I could choose to terminate the pregnancy.

I left that appointment in disbelief and shock. *Why couldn't this motherhood thing be easy for me? Like I had seen for so many other people.*

But then, I felt my baby kick. That kick jolted me from going down a path of reality that was not mine, and connected me to the one that was.

I walked into my doctor's office the next day, deeply connected in faith and love, and refused the amniocentesis. Whatever the future held for us was ours.

And then a miracle happened. He told me about this new non-invasive test that had come out the day before called Harmony. It was a simple blood draw, but because the test was new, it would take two weeks for results. Larry and I were the second couple to receive the test in all of Alberta.

During those two weeks, I grounded myself in daily meditation. I didn't push my fears away. Rather, I allowed them to come up during meditation and met them without judgment and expectation. I met them with love instead.

By the time we received the call with the results, I had felt so grounded in love that fear had nowhere to grow.

The tests revealed that she did not have the condition that concerned the doctor.

As I neared the end of my pregnancy, I found myself being pulled again. The thoughts of losing my daughter gripped me. Thoughts of death lurked in the shadows, keeping me up at night.

Instead of enjoying her movement and feeling her life, I would count her kicks, waiting for her death. I would yearn for the time when she was no longer inside, hidden in darkness. I wanted her in my arms—in the safety of daylight. I had convinced myself that once she was born, all my worry, fear, and anxiety would dissolve.

Boy, was I wrong.

After thirty-six hours of labor and an emergency C-section, it was more than an hour before I got to hold my child in the safety of my arms. I was strapped down to a bed in the recovery area, looking at her, my whole body yearning to feel her skin against mine. To smell her hair. To kiss her soft toes.

Finally, when my vitals were back to normal, they placed my daughter in my arms. I had dreamed of that moment for two years—but it didn't feel safe. I fumbled around trying to hold her wriggling body as I struggled to breastfeed.

Nothing about motherhood seemed natural or easy.

I allowed fear to take over.

I had once again become completely disconnected from myself and my reality.

From love.

Hardly anyone noticed the disconnection. They saw a mom finally holding a live, healthy baby and assumed the tears and doting were normal.

But there was nothing normal about my situation.

The morning of my daughter's first birthday, I woke up and looked around. I saw her running down the hallway and into her dad's arms. I really looked at her. And for the first time, I truly saw *her*. Not the milestones that I had been so worried over. Not her weight. Not how much she slept or how much she ate.

I saw *her*. Every glorious brown curl that touched her cheek. Her strong legs that had her walking at nine months. Her glorious laugh that made everyone around her burst into laughter as well.

I realized at that moment that I had missed out on truly seeing my daughter. I had missed out on the first year of her life because I was so deeply pulled by fear.

Even if my pregnancy with my daughter resulted in loss, I would have wanted to experience the joy, connection, and love in the journey.

From that day, I found myself on a healing path, unlike anything I had ever experienced.

I finally became present enough to see that my fear-provoking thoughts had become detrimental to me and my family's well-being. I needed to do something.

I recalled the night I straddled both life and death, waiting for my second baby to pass through me.

Sometimes you have to lose everything in order to regain yourself.

I knew I had to lose all my old conditioning to regain and get to know myself without fear,and learn to manage my thoughts.

I met thoughts mindfully and in love so that they had the space to transform into something else.

I believe this simple, yet powerful practice of meditation and mindfulness truly saved my life.

The loss of pregnancies, babies, and dreams changed me. It changed every aspect of me. It changed how I move through this world, how I experience life, and how I parent.

I was undeniably different. I see now that I needed to be.

I left my career in social work to pursue my dream of supporting other women as they moved through the complex journey of motherhood. I never wanted another woman to be so deeply pulled by fear, as I had. I didn't want another mother to wake up a year later and realize she missed everything: her pregnancy, moments, and her *life*.

The universe guided me when I learned that a dear friend of mine had received a poor prenatal diagnosis at twenty-one weeks pregnant.

As I sat with my friend when she birthed her daughter, Willa, silently into the world, it became clear to me that I was put in that room for a purpose.

It made me create my business, Pregnancy Loss Healing. A business which allows me to help other women root back to love through the journey of loss.

Love and loss are continuously weaving in and out of life. It is in loss that we can choose to root ourselves back to love. It is a conscious choice that we make every day, in every moment.

Today, I am blessed to raise my one living child who is transgender, a beautiful soul who has taught me so much. Through pregnancy loss to navigating the complex emotions of parenting a transgender boy, I have allowed myself to feel on my own terms. I have allowed myself to stay connected. Instead of fear, I continue to root back to love; root back to me.

Moment to moment.

Day by day.

Despite it being hard.

And scary.

I choose love.

Lessons Learned:

1) Your thoughts are not real. Don't let your mind convince you that the worst-case scenario will always occur.

2) Meditation, though simple, can be one of the most powerful acts of self-love. Give yourself permission to get to know yourself; she's been waiting.

3) There is no life *after* loss but rather life *with* loss. Loss changes you—it's not about how you get over it but how you learn to honor and live alongside loss.

Mindset Tips:

1) Feel Your feelings. The only way to get through any challenge is to go *through* it. You cannot numb yourself or try to quickly carry on without first allowing yourself to *fee*l. Allow all your feelings to show up without trying to block or change them. Feeling your emotions won't do anything except allow them the space to transform into something else.

2) Ask for support. Reach out to trusted friends and family, or a coach that specializes in pregnancy or infant loss. Reaching out for support doesn't make you weak, it will make you stronger.

3) You will be different—but it doesn't have to be for the worse. The truth is losing a pregnancy and a baby is life changing and you will be undeniably changed. With some help, inner reflection, and time to grieve you can learn to move through your triggers, rediscover your strength, and connect with a deep sense of self love. Your loss can grow you into a more compassionate, empathetic and present person if you allow it. So, you will be different but different does not always equal worse.

Aha Moments and Self Reflection

Note your Thoughts

Danielle Lynn

Danielle Lynn, originally from New Castle Pennsylvania, resides in East Palestine, Ohio with her husband. With nineteen years social work and counseling experience, Danielle earned a Bachelor of Science degree through Slippery Rock University, and holds a Master's in Social Work through the University of Pittsburgh. She is currently an addictions counselor in Pennsylvania as well as a bestselling author on Amazon.

Danielle had her first solo publishing in 2019 with an Inspiration Planner, focusing on the teachings of gratitude. With these publishings Danielle has reconnected with her Alumni Slippery Rock University, having her publishings featured in the University bookstore. Danielle's publishings can also be found at Leana's Bookstore in Hermitage, Pennsylvania.

Even with a busy career, Danielle has many hobbies and interest. She enjoys being outdoors, spending time with her family and close friends, relaxing with her pets, antiquing, woodworking, reading, writing, cooking, and taking motorcycle rides with her husband.

Connect with Danielle:

4daniellelynn@gmail.com

www.daniellelynninspires.com

fb.me/44daniellelynn

www.Instagram.com/dschotzie

Chapter 9

Dreams Do Come True

By Danielle Lynn

Imagine being in the third grade, sitting at your desk, in the classroom. Your teacher calls you to the front of the room to question you about the obvious.

The obvious, in my case, was something she had noticed about my report card, one of those yellow cardstock report cards. The obvious was that I had used white-out on my yellow report card to change my grade. Guilty. The obvious flaw noticed by every adult who reviewed my report card. The obvious edit that my father questioned me about; I still remember that conversation. I was obviously in trouble. I would have felt embarrassed anyway but, as an overachiever, I felt especially ashamed to have earned a D in reading. Yes, reading.

It was eventually discovered that I had a reading comprehension problem, something I struggle with to this day. Interestingly, as a result, writing became my strength instead of my weakness. I learned that writing could be my outlet for explaining my feelings and ideas thoroughly. Writing is how I learned to study, pass exams, and take home report cards with A's and B's rather than C's and D's.

Writing empowered me to express myself fully. When I was in elementary school, I fell in love with Judy Bloom's books. Getting lost in the stories, envisioning the characters, and relating to the events were my favorite parts of reading her books. Now, I love telling my own stories and offering them up for others to get lost in, as I once did in Judy Bloom's.

Let's Get Personal

I never would have imagined myself as an entrepreneur. My tendency was always to play it safe; in my mind being an entrepreneur was not safe. I had already overcome so many obstacles in life and I knew that I would continue to face challenges an entrepreneur, but when the time came, I decided to take the leap anyway. It really went against the grain; I do *not* like not having control over areas that personally affect me. Being a counselor really helped me understand exactly why that is.

I did not have a bad upbringing. My family was close and included cousins, aunts, uncles, and grandparents that were very active in my life. I remember feeling wanted and loved. I still feel wanted and loved.

I have always been an overachiever with a Type A personality, the result of both natural disposition and upbringing. Not only was I naturally driven to excel, but my parents also set high standards for me when I was growing up. It's not that I felt pressured, but they encouraged me to become a responsible, caring adult. I am grateful for their efforts and their dedication to our family.

I have encountered many obstacles and experienced many drawbacks in life, from divorce and multiple pregnancy losses to automobile accidents, assaults, and toxic relationships. As you can imagine, I have found that resiliency is essential for overcoming hardship and encouraging growth. I would not have become the person I am today without it.

Relationships are important. As human beings, we are social, we seek connection, and we crave acceptance by our group of choice. When they are healthy, relationships are wonderful but what happens when they turn toxic? We all have some experience with difficult relationships; it's inevitable. They can develop anywhere: work, among family and friends, even with our own spouse. The tricky part is recognizing the situation before it becomes a problem. Learning to let go of toxic relationships and developing more awareness around them has been one of my biggest challenges.

Toxicity often develops out of unreasonable expectations and can deteriorate into negative, abusive situations. It can also manifest in more subtle ways. Think of the relationships in your life. Do people sometimes place unreasonable demands on you as a condition for getting along? Are you always reasonable in your expectations of others? In a healthy relationship of any kind, everyone must manage their expectations.

I have learned that not everyone shares my interests, for example. I avoid taking it personally if someone shows little interest in my business. When a person's body language, or general lack of attention, is telling me that they are not into what I am talking about, I know I have to respect that. I just can't expect everyone to be as into my entrepreneurial journey as I am, no matter how enthusiastic and positive I feel about it. That's okay. I have learned to be selective when it comes to the people I choose to share my new career with. It's been an interesting process. So, if you want to avoid toxic relationships, start by not letting the expectations of others control you and don't push your own expectations on them.

It has been said that you are most like the five people you are closest to. Based on my own experience, I can attest to the truth of that statement.

My closest relationship today is with my best friend who also happens to be my husband. As a couple, we are like a single unit: we communicate with just a look, we have similar mannerisms, and we share inside jokes. That being said, we have also retained our own separate identities and personalities.

When my husband and I first met, we bonded over the shared experience of having endured a failed marriage. We related to each other's frustrations and feelings. Being able to turn to him was a huge relief because he understood my feelings, my anger, and my disappointment in another human being.

It is not uncommon for relationships to develop out of shared experience, that's how it was for us. In this case, there was a positive outcome because we started with mutual respect, support, and friendship.

The end of other relationships opened the door for my husband to enter my life. Now he is not just part of my life, he *is* my life. Consider why you are connected to certain individuals. There is a reason that they are in your life. That reason can either be healthy or unhealthy. That is for you to decide.

You will always have problems, but don't let them become your focus.

Building and developing new relationships is all part of being a successful entrepreneur. Since I am now able to identify how important relationships are *to* me and *for* me, I try to follow my instinct when it comes to people I *want* and *need* to work with.

I have worked with MLM companies for nearly ten years, and one thing I can tell you about selling someone else's products is that it is a struggle. Something that I have learned about developing my own brand, however, is that I can sell myself and my brand 100 percent. People want to hear what I have to say. They want to see what I am going to do next. They reach out to me and tell me what an influence I have been on their lives. It is wonderful.

What they don't know, unless they are also entrepreneurs, is just how difficult it can be to connect with others. It can be so hard to find your tribe and support network. There are times when you feel completely alone. It is very important to connect with the right people so you can develop a solid support system and find compatible business partners. It is not enough for them to be in business, they also have to share your interests and worldview. In my experience, connecting with the right people makes all the difference.

The opportunity to become a published author came along "by chance" with one of my current publishers. We were both in a paid-membership online group of fellow entrepreneurs. I was interested in publishing my own planner and began to look into my options.

While I was developing the planner, I was introduced to another publisher who was looking for contributors to her latest compilation. I immediately felt comfortable with both publishers and wanted to join their teams. I also wanted them on *my* team. They both seemed to genuinely care about what I was trying to do and they understood my vision.

My contribution to the compilation was very personal and covered the numerous losses I had experienced in less than a years' time, including a miscarriage, a divorce, losing my position as a school social worker, losing my home, and filing for bankruptcy. Thanks to the success of that publication, I became a bestselling author in

March of 2018 and my books are now featured in stores including my alma mater's bookstore.

My experience with each publication was very different and this is when I began to recognize how resilient I really am. The compilation book succeeded beyond expectations, reaching Number One in three categories, while my *Inspirational Planner* failed to launch on time because of printing complications. The delay caused me great stress and frustration, especially because this was my first solo publication. My planner was eventually released on Amazon but not until five months after the official launch date; I was extremely disappointed.

In both cases, regardless of the outcome, I worked diligently on marketing and on increasing my visibility. I did not let a failed online launch affect what I could control. I was completely new to the book world and sought advice from both publishers to get the most out of both publications.

Connecting with people was one thing that came easy to me. So, I decided to launch the planner myself, even though the book was still on hold with Amazon. I reached out to community members, friends, and family, and made it happen. I had spent a lot of time online observing women entrepreneurs achieve success; I never thought that I could do it myself. But I did. I arranged my own launch and people actually showed up.

Connecting and speaking with others, as simple as that may sound, worked. Now, I have women reaching out to me, personally, asking, "How did you do that? How are you doing all of this with a full-time job?" They have noticed that I *am* making things happen!

Visibility and Marketing

Visibility is to be seen. Being seen is to be known. And I want to be known. I want to be known as a woman who helps other women to connect. I would love to create an online network of women entrepreneurs who empower, support, and guide one another. If not for the Internet, I would never have found the support necessary to become a published author. Now I am visible to the whole world, thanks to Facebook, Instagram, and Amazon.

These days, online networking is a necessary if you want to increase brand visibility. And building healthy relationships is essential for achieving overall success. I never used to believe that "success is about who you know and not what you know", but I feel that I am living proof that making the right connections at the right time can make all the difference. The guidance and support I've received from the powerhouse women I have met, has been invaluable. It's important to find the right people - people you can relate to and who are high achievers, even overachievers.

The Internet is not the only place you can market your brand, however. I have also made sure that I am visible to my community: local store owners, friends, and family in Pennsylvania and Ohio.

In March 2018, the compilation book *Your Shift Matters* became a number one bestseller on Amazon. At that time, I began reaching out to community members for book signings. My goal was to share these inspirational stories and help people understand the importance of learning from the successes and failure of others.

I reached out to the local businesses in my town as well as the library. The owner of the Main Street Shop in Columbiana, Ohio, was happy to let me use her country-antique store, so we set up two events and promoted them as book signings with a local author. I remember feeling excited and nervous at the same time: excited to try something new and be part of a bestselling book, nervous about the reception I would get. I was also worried about whether anyone would show up. Thankfully, I was not disappointed: the events were well attended, and I met some amazing people.

In the fall of 2018, I reconnected with my alma mater, Slippery Rock University. The university was very supportive, even featuring my book in the SGA bookstore. It was an amazing experience to go back to where I earned a college degree and see my work on display in the school's store. It is hard to describe my feelings of complete happiness and surprise. Even now, I still have the biggest smile on my face whenever I walk into the SGA Bookstore.

After making arrangements with the university, I decided to go visit a local store, book in hand. I had no appointment, but I asked to speak to someone about displaying my work. As it turns out, I was speaking to the owner of Leana's Books & More. The conversation was so natural and easy that we signed a contract right then and there. At that moment, I really knew what pure joy felt like.

Not everyone I asked said yes, but, with more yesses than noes, I was already more successful than I could ever have imagined. Even better, the yesses I got, turned out to be for the right locations and from the right people.

Along the way, I learned a few things about myself and about succeeding as an entrepreneur:

1) I like who I am: I do not like to fail, I am resilient, I am stubborn, I am helpful, I am dedicated, I have a huge heart, I have a voice.

2) An entrepreneur should never be afraid to ask.

3) You *will* find helpers along the way: there are always people in this world that want to help others and are genuinely happy to see them succeed.

We all have our gifts. We all have our talents. We all have our failings. We all have our frustrations. Each of our stories is unique because we are all unique individuals. We are our own experts because our stories are about our own experiences. Discover and rediscover yourself, your gifts, and your talents. Trust what you find and use that knowledge to make your mark.

Failure is a part of life. To achieve success, you must turn your failures into something positive. Use your failures to teach as well as to learn. Use them to push yourself and to help others along the way. Do not let the bad times hold you back. Only *you* know what you want achieve in life. So, if you have not been living, start now!

Lessons Learned:

1) Don't be afraid to ask. If you need help, ask. If you want to be involved, ask. If you need clarity, ask. If you do not ask, the answer will always be, "no".
2) The keys to success are mindset, growth, hard work, and staying true to your values.
3) Always go for your personal best and you will experience ultimate happiness.

Mindset Tips:

1) Self-care is necessary: schedule time for yourself often; relax your mind and body.
2) Build self-confidence: believe in yourself, trust that you are capable, and remember to be yourself.
3) Appreciate where you are: be grateful in mind and gracious in life.

Aha Moments and Self Reflection

Note your Thoughts

Karen Gedney MD

Karen Gedney MD, ABAARM is board certified in both internal medicine and anti-aging regenerative medicine. As a National Health Service Corps Scholarship winner, she was placed in a male medium security prison after her training, to do a four-year payback in 1987. Against all the odds, she turned it into a calling that lasted almost three decades.

She was given The Nevada Hero's for Humanity Award in 2000 for her work as a pioneer in HIV care in correctional settings. Karen was also recognized by the American Correctional Association as one of the 'Best in the Business'.

On leaving the prison in 2016, Karen dedicated her life as a catalyst to shift the current prison paradigm to one of prevention, healing and re-integration. Her first book is her memoir, 30 Years Behind Bars, Trials of a Prison Doctor and is available on her website and on Amazon.

Connect with Karen online:

https://www.discoverdrg.com/

https://www.facebook.com/KarenGedneyMD/

https://twitter.com/KarenGedney_DrG

Chapter 10

Thirty Years Behind Bars

By Karen Gedney

Why do some people look at adversity and think of it as a painful setback, while others think of it as a unique opportunity?

I've always been curious about why people have such different responses to the same event. How much of their response is due to their biology, their environment or other variables?

I don't think it's any surprise that I ended up straddling two worlds that gave me the ability to study that question. Those two were the world of medicine and the prison world.

In 1987, I completed my internal medicine residency and was placed in a male medium security prison in Nevada to do a four-year payback for a medical school scholarship that I had received. By that time I had overcome a variety of obstacles to become a doctor, but I didn't fathom the obstacles I would encounter as a prison doctor.

Prisons are designed to incarcerate, punish and shame. They label and classify inmates based on the worst thing they have ever done in their lives, and they are not oriented to understand, heal or give them hope. My temperament, training, and orientation were the exact opposite. I wanted to understand why they had made the decisions in life that had ruined their health, their lives, and other people's lives, and put their future in the free world at risk. I wanted to help heal not only the symptoms, but also the root cause of what caused the symptoms in the first place. I wanted also to do it with compassion and with attention to what they would need when and if they re-entered society.

When you find yourself in an organization, a business or a relationship where you have a diametrically opposite viewpoint and agenda, adversity is soon to follow. It didn't take long for me to realize that fact, but as a new doctor in an alien world, I was not sure what to do. The most reasonable thing would have been to go to my supervisor, but that person left due to illness. I didn't have a supervisor to ask, and one wasn't put in place for over a year.

The second reasonable thing to expect in a prison environment would be some in-service training. That did not happen. In fact, on my first day of the job I was not told that the man leading me around in a blue scrub suit was an inmate, not a member of staff.

My first year was one of survival and trying to figure out the rules, the hierarchy, and whom I could trust. I could trust that the inmates wanted something from me to make their lives more bearable, whether it was easing a medical problem, an emotional problem or a problem they were having with the prison system.

I was unclear whom I could trust in the non-inmate population that ran the prison. I knew that some individuals in positions of power resented me, because they believed in the adage, "lock them up and throw away the key, they've got nothin' comin'." I knew others looked at me and saw my compassion and wanting to help the inmates as a weakness, and even a security risk.

A year had not passed before I started to hear that I was under investigation by the inspector general's office. I had heard that a state worker could be let go if they did not pass their probationary period, which was one year. My paranoid mind went into a spin, and the vortex sucked me down into a well of every imaginable horrible outcome.

1) The state would kick me out of the site the National Health Service Corps had placed me in to do a four-year payback. Which meant that if I couldn't do the payback, I would be fined three times the amount of my full medical school scholarship. That meant I would be in debt my entire life.
2) They would charge me with something and strip me of my medical license that I had worked for my entire life.
3) They would do something that would cause my marriage to go on the rocks, and my husband would leave me.

Working in a negative environment, where everyone around me seemed to look for the worst in people, rubbed off on me and fed my paranoid thoughts. I heard rumors and stories of what they did to people they wanted to get rid of, and I needed to do something besides waiting. I turned to the one person I did trust, my husband, Clifton.

He told me to go to my supervisor. I didn't have one. Then he said, "Who's in charge of the prison system?" I responded, "I guess the prison director."

That's how I ended up in the director's office looking at files that stood a good eight inches tall with the words, 'Inspector General' stamped across them. The director pushed them toward me and said, "I never do this, but you need to know your enemies and get them before they get you."

When I read what people said about me, I had to bite the inside of my check to not let the stinging behind my eyes result in tears. A tremendous amount that was said about me was taken out of context, but a fair amount could be said to be outright misogyny and racism. I happened to be a tall, athletic, blonde, thirty-one year old, married to a tall, muscular forty-three-year-old, intelligent, black male in a place that had less than a 0.1% black population. That city of about 40,000 stood in contrast to the three prisons on its outskirts, which had a black population of twenty-five percent.

When the prison director told me, "Get them, before they get you," I was unable to wrap my brain around that tactic. I asked, "Why don't you take care of them?"

He said, "They've got something on me."

What type of adverse world was this? I still had another three years to go to complete my payback for the scholarship. What was I going to do? The director made it clear to me what he thought of the files when he tossed them in the wastebasket, but I still felt like I was a small boat on a rough sea with the clouds darkening.

I had a choice; I could act like a victim and let the storm sink me, or I could chart my course and play to my strengths. My strength was the medical world, not the correctional world, and there was no shortage of medical problems in the prison.

One of the first medical problems I tackled when I entered the prison was the rate of HIV and AIDS among patients. When I walked through those prison gates on my first day, AIDS was a death sentence and AZT, the first medication for HIV, had not yet been released. Nevada, as a state, was unique in that it made the decision to test every inmate in the prison for HIV in 1985. What was not unique was that they had no idea what to do with the information. They had no strategy regarding who was told, who received the information, how the inmate would be classified and treated, and who would receive education on HIV.

As a doctor, I had no meds to stop them from dying from HIV. However, I did have the ability to act in a different way. I started the first HIV support group in the prison yard and told them how to keep their immune systems as strong as possible, how not to infect others and why reaching out for support and keeping hope alive was so vital to their battle.

I also realized that the inmates were not the only ones frightened. There were doctors in the community who were afraid and didn't want to deal with them. There were custody officers so scared they would be infected by the slightest non-blood interaction with an HIV infected inmate that they never took off their plastic gloves.

There was a lot of fear and adversity surrounding AIDS in the 1980s. It was also a time of great opportunity to become part of the solution vs. blaming, ostracizing, ignoring or hiding. Instead of getting upset with the officers who over-reacted or said the inmates 'deserved it', I chose to develop an educational class on HIV. They turned me down at first, but I was able to convince the training officer for the new custody staff to let me teach about 'blood precautions', where I taught them not only about hepatitis, but HIV as well.

I could have stopped there on HIV and waited till a drug came out, but I became involved in learning as much as I could about the disease and what drug companies were trying to accomplish. My interest in that area gave me a unique opportunity to become a leader in HIV care in the correctional world as well as a speaker at a national level. Those emotional experiences watching young men die when I had no medications that would help them, followed by watching HIV go from a death sentence to a manageable chronic disease during my career, will forever be with me.

Emotional experiences that follow adversity tend to stick in one's mind. One can change how we interpret those expereinces after we've processed them, and that's where one of the opportunities can exist.

When I'm asked what was the worst thing that ever happened to me in prison, October, Friday the 13th 1989, pops into my mind. The prison gates clanged behind me as I walked that morning to my office, which doubled as an exam room at the end of a long hallway. My first patient that morning was an inmate they called, Moth. I had seen him several times in the past for minor medical problems and psychological issues related to the killing he did as a marine in Vietnam. When he returned from war, he was unable to re-integrate into society and ended up robbing a bank and killing a state trooper. He had been in prison for fourteen years and knew he had no hope of ever leaving, because he had been given a life sentence with no possibility of parole. The years of incarceration weighed on him and made him look old and gray, like a moth, even though he was only in his forties.

That morning he assaulted me in my office and took me hostage. I was shocked and angry. How dare he do that to me when I was only trying to help him as a doctor? But it wasn't that simple. He had started to see me as more than a doctor. He looked at me as an object of his desire and all the things that he would never have or possess in life again. He could not stand that, nor the thought of spending his life in what he considered hell. He was too narcissistic to consider suicide, but forcing their hand to kill him made sense. I was raped four hours into the ten-hour ordeal, before a swat team got me out with a concussion grenade and killed Moth, a few feet from me.

I returned to work the following workday, which was Monday. No one from the prison system had checked how I was doing over the weekend, and it was obvious to me that they were not expecting me back that Monday. They had not fixed the hole in the wall where they had sledgehammered a kick out panel before tossing in the grenade, and the room was freezing.

However, there was one group who asked how I was doing—the inmates. Every time they saw me in those first few weeks, they wanted me to know they cared, and they sent me dozens of get-well cards. Forty-three lifers—men who would never leave prison—signed a card. They showed me compassion, and they helped me heal.

Everyone reacts differently to events like the one I lived through on Friday the 13th. Some thought I was tough and "had balls" when I went right back to work. Some thought I should take off time and sue the prison for not protecting me. Others thought I needed "help."

I didn't have "balls." I had a German mother who had instilled in me to be conscientious and not make any excuses for not doing the work I was supposed to do. She and my father also believed in not being weak, a victim or looking for handouts. Getting "help" would be considered a weakness, but I decided to talk to a psychiatrist after I noticed that I was coming down with a number of colds after the event, which was very unusual for me. I knew that my body was telling me what my mind was trying to avoid, and that was that maybe I did need some "help."

Asking for help was difficult for me. It was an obstacle that I usually avoided and would rationalize by telling myself that I could handle it on my own or that I didn't want to bother someone. I knew it was an obstacle and it took me a while to convince myself that going to a psychiatrist would be a unique opportunity and that I might learn something. First, I had to find someone in the community who I didn't know, was not a pill pusher, and was considered sane. That was not easy, but I was fortunate enough to find a female psychiatrist who listened to my story and picked up on the fact that I had not resolved my anger over what happened. In essence, she gave me permission to feel my anger, deal with it and let it go.

I was not only angry at Moth. I was angry with myself for not seeing that he would take his pain out on me. I was angry that custody had allowed it to happen, and on some level, I thought that custody wanted to see me get hurt. I was angry that the system did not show me compassion after the event. I had a lot of anger, and I realized that my ability to allow myself to feel it, talk about it and let it go was something that did not come naturally. I thought I was good at controlling my emotions, but what I was good at was disconnecting myself from emotions that I did not want to feel. They came out, though, in the disguise of irritation, frustration, and a reduced immune system to colds.

That insight helped me overcome my greatest obstacle to healing, and allowed me to do something constructive with my anger. I didn't know how important that insight was until I was teaching the class for the new officers on bloodborne diseases and HIV in the prison. I always asked them if they had any questions and, in one class, a new female officer raised her hand and said, "Dr. Gedney, we heard you were taken hostage, can you tell us what it was like?"

It was the first time anyone in the world of custody had ever talked to me about the hostage incident. That poor class, I emotionally vomited all over them. In the midst of it though, I realized the most important piece. I never wanted them to experience it, and if they did experience trauma in the prison, I wanted their co-workers and system to act compassionately and learn from the event.

Adversity and obstacles are much easier to overcome when that hard-won knowledge is shared, so others don't make the same mistake. That poor class was not expecting my raw emotion. Some had tears in their eyes, and others recoiled. I was fortunate that the officer who was in charge of training had been in the military and had an education higher than the average new hire with a high school diploma. He came up to me after the class and told me that the new officers needed to hear what I had to say. He also told me it would help me. He was right. I was able to process all those emotions—now it is simply a story.

A story. One of the things that I have always known is that people remember stories that elicit emotion. They don't remember statistics, numbers, charts or spreadsheets. They also tend not to remember regulations, rules, and warnings, especially if they don't like them.

When I look back on my life, I think of the stories I read as a child that captured my imagination and put me on the path to be a doctor. There were no stories about doctors who worked in prisons and had to deal with the adversity and obstacles that I experienced.

I ended up not only surviving my four-year payback for medical school but also made the decision to stay in the prison and turn it into my calling. I spent thirty years doing what I could on the inside to shift the prison paradigm toward one of trying to understand behavior and relieve suffering, versus harming and making someone more dangerous when they left prison.

There are many who work in prison that are affected by the negative environment and the stress of always expecting the worst out of people. They tend to count their days to retirement like an inmate counting the days to their release. There are others, though, who don't take things personally, have a flexible mindset, and believe that people can change. Instead of counting the days to retirement, that group tends to think before reacting and looks for ways to support programs that are known to reduce violence or recidivism.

Looking back has made me realize that it was the obstacles and adversity I experienced as a naïve young doctor that gave me unique opportunities to personally grow and make an impact in a truly underserved area of medicine—prisons. I also came to understand that treating a medical problem wasn't enough for me. I also had to understand and address the behavior that led to the health problem in the first place. That propelled me to develop programs as a volunteer in the evening. They ranged from courses like health-related recovery to help the inmates with their addictive behavior to Toastmasters where they could learn to communicate what they wanted to say in front of a group of people, like the parole board.

When I finally walked through those prison gates for the last time as their doctor, I still felt that I was not done. How could I help them from outside the prison walls? Retirement was not necessarily an obstacle. I could now turn my attention to help them re-enter society by supporting organizations that help inmates with housing and wraparound services like counseling and help with employment. That is how I ended up being on the board for the Ridge House in Reno, which gives those opportunities to inmates leaving the prison. Organizations like the Ridge House for inmates are rare, though, and have beds for only a small number of inmates.

I helped to make a real difference, not only in re-entry, but in shifting the paradigm of prisons from punishment, harm, and recidivism to healing and re-integration. My paradigm of what was possible as a child shifted when I was exposed to stories about doctors and healers that saved people who others had abandoned. Those stories resonated with me, and I envisioned myself in that role, which gave me a sense of purpose and the ability to get through the bad times and look back at them as a learning experience.

What story could I share that could help shift the prison paradigm to one that would keep society safer? I've been told it's the power of the personal story that makes all the difference and I certainly have one. It's my memoir, *30 Years Behind Bars*.

Addendum:

On December 6, 2018, I flew into Las Vegas, NV to attend the Razor Wire exhibition, curated by Shaun T. Griffin that featured art and poetry from the Razor Wire Poetry Workshop. The workshop was held at the Northern Nevada Correctional center that I worked at for thirty years. It was at the Nevada Humanities Program Gallery, and I picked up one of the Razor Wire poetry journals on the display table from 1992. Those journals were published every year for the last thirty years. I leafed through the journal and spotted an inmate's name that I knew very well from the past. Someone I knew had died a few years after he left prison. His name was Stephen Fogarty and the poem that caught my eye was called *Ode to a Lady Prison Doctor*. I was the only female prison doctor at that time.

Through

white

light,

burning

bright

and

soft,

the

kind

a

man

sees

perched

on the

edge

of

eternity,

steps

fine,

angel-haired

Madonna

with

body-mending

hands

and

heart-healing

spirit

into

a world

dark

with

deprivation

she cries:

weighted

and

shackled

by the

pain

of

a

place

where

never

she belonged.

Lessons Learned:

1) Realize that emotions are contagious and when you are negatively affected by adverse circumstances do not feed that contagion with your negative emotions.
2) Find one positive thing to do that has you looking ahead vs staying stuck in the past.
3) Listen to your body. If your health starts to change in a negative way remember that emotions like chronic stress, anger, depression, resentment, and sadness take a toll not only on your body, but your ability to deal with adversity.

Mindset Tips:

1) Have a flexible mind set and embrace, enjoy, and take part in where you want change to take us.
2) Be curious, not judgmental.
3) Keep your sense of humor and above all else be able to laugh at yourself.

Aha Moments and Self Reflection

Note your Thoughts

Tracy Rickards

Tracy initially created the *Kiss Your Boss Goodbye* book, coaching and online training course, to free herself from a corporate job that was killing her soul.

Tracy's rediscovery of herself and becoming the master of her own world was fueled by a surprising sequence of events. Her quest for learning, fulfillment, and to have it all 'make sense' was her catalyst to freedom and living her ultimate dream. As a speaker and educator, she provides a powerful combination of the business and personal skills you require to transform your life with confidence.

Being an advocate for self-discovery, personal fulfillment, and standing apart from the crowd, Tracy boldly and candidly shares her years of education and experience. Becoming the master of your destiny does not have to take years – transformation and freedom are only one decision away.

Connect with Tracy:

https://www.facebook.com/tracyrickards.sassysuccess/

https://www.tracyrickards.com

https://www.connectwithtracy.com

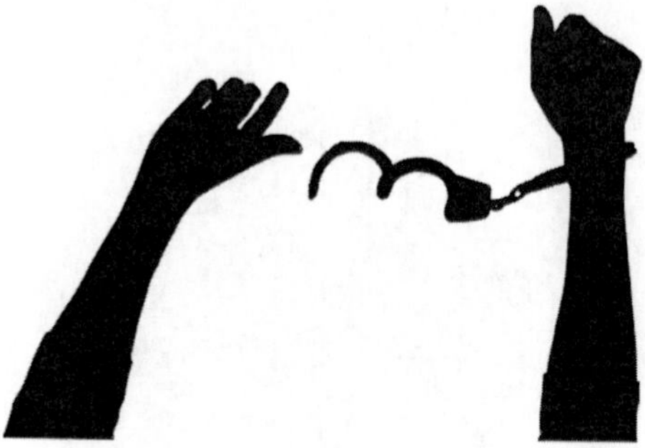

Chapter 11

I was in Prison

By Tracy Rickards

My cell was larger than average, and I had newer furnishings than the others. It was often cold; the warmth from the old boiler-style heater sporadically formed a wall between me and the outside world.

But at least I had a window.

I could see off in the distance the hubbub of city life. On clear days I could see much further, to the mountainous region of the Northwest. On days that were severely smokey from the ravaging forest fires, I could only imagine that other world—the one I couldn't touch.

Day after day, I spent my time alone. The walls seemed to close in around me, save for the odd visitor who stopped in. Usually when people came to me, it was mostly for what I could do for *them*. It was not often reciprocated. When I needed help, it seemed they rarely had the time or desire. Maybe no one actually *could* provide what I needed. I was, after all, a leader and protector. How could anyone respect me if I showed weakness?

The gang-culture was very distinct. Each belonged to their own territory defined by skillsets and job type, but also divided in race and ethnicity. I thought myself to be someone who could fit in anywhere, but certain groups just weren't willing to let me in.

At least it wasn't violent, just the hushed chortles of laughter and gossip behind my back. It was hard to tell who was really a friend and who wasn't. The only choice was to simply trust people from a distance. "Keep your friends close and your enemies closer," as the adage goes.

After a period of time, I received special privileges—I was moved between two facilities monthly. It broke up the scheduled monotony. The travel provided new scenery and some actual conversation for a time. The smells were different. The food was better.

The tension, however, was still the same; maybe even worse. I had to establish myself in the new culture—the new and unfamiliar environment—while maintaining my status at the old one. Some were jealous. Others viewed me as a brown noser, further alienating me and making me a target for abuse.

Then there was the "management." Different rules, different policies and different expectations, and none of them written down. Inconsistent rules made it hard for me to tell how I was supposed to handle myself. I was just supposed to *know*.

It was a world where I was damned if I did and damned if I didn't. I was surrounded by other prisoners feeling the exact same way, yet afraid to speak up. They refused to show weakness, lest they become the next one victimized and terrorized by the mob and class mentality.

Yes, I was in prison—but this was Corporate America. I signed up for a life of doing what I was told. Directed when to show up, when to leave, when to take breaks, when I would be traveling, who to reward, who to punish, how to think and how to speak.

But at least I had a window….

Turning Point

I had a decent paycheque, benefits, and a company credit card. I answered only to the president. From the outside, it appeared I had it all. Secretly though, I felt trapped. I wore a gleaming set of "Golden Handcuffs:" The illusion of security keeping my butt firmly planted in my office chair.

The turning point came one day under the guise of a shaved, balding head and patent leather shoes. Instead of the one boss who was nearly impossible to follow, I now had two—and they were at odds with each other. I felt squeezed in between. The more I pulled away from my job emotionally and physically, the more I felt pulled back in to make it *somehow* work. I had invested fifteen years in the company: watched it grow, fed it, and nurtured it as I had my own children. I had a great team that I loved. To walk away from the salary, benefits, and company card? Was I crazy?

The more I wanted out, the more fearful I became of *actually* leaving. It felt like a Chinese finger puzzle of epic proportion. It was a torturous decision.

But one day, I found the strength and courage to pull the pin. It didn't happen overnight. It took a lot of painful experiences, a few lonely years, and a deep journey into myself to finally make my escape a reality.

How Did I Get Here?

Becoming an accountant for me was serendipitous, more by accident that by choice, but I can now see how it all came together.

Through every experience, every job, every hardship, I was being groomed for something different.

I grew up in a very small town in British Columbia, Canada where there was no mall, no movie theaters, and no library. I had to travel to neighboring towns to go to school. There were few choices for a girl with my interests. My options included all things outdoorsy: hunting, fishing, baseball, camping, gardening—NOTHING for me, except swimming in the river for a month or two in summer.

I wanted to learn! Explore the world! Solve great mysteries! I lost myself in school and books, favoring *Encyclopedia Brown*, *The Hardy Boys*, and *Harriet the Spy*. On weekends I loved the old Perry Mason reruns, and anything with lawyers, cops and robbers.

At eight years old, I decided I would be a prosecuting attorney when I grew up. Instead of being encouraged to pursue my dreams, I was met with "You can't do that. That's not for people like us. That's for someone in the *big* city."

So, I set my sights on the "Big City." Problem solved.

I only had to get through the next *nine* years of school to be able to make my dreams come true, to finally get something *I* wanted—and to be happy. *What could go wrong?*

I made friends easily. I joined clubs like 4H Sewing, Air Cadets, and was continually elected to Student Council. This gave me my first experience with leadership and public speaking, activities I enjoyed.

Learning came easily to me, so I was bored out of my mind at school. My solace was hanging out with friends, talking, and listening to music. It wasn't long until we found alcohol to brighten our spirits and dull our senses. I also found it as a way to numb the emptiness I felt inside.

I was very aware of the deep black hole within me, but blind to the journey it would take to fill it. Boredom and early experimentation is a really bad mix for a young teenage girl. Unplanned, I became pregnant at fifteen.

Stalled in my tracks and unsure what to do, I procrastinated for two full weeks to tell my parents. Before I could, tragedy struck. My grandfather, "Papa", passed away. I couldn't tell them now! I waited a further two weeks. The emotional turmoil was crippling, but I wore my mask very well.

As an A-student, I dropped out of school in Grade 10 while pregnant. I attempted correspondence school, but just could not get motivated. Being at home alone studying was not the same as the fun we had learning at school.

In May, my beautiful son was born. I had just turned sixteen. With his dad, we moved into a tiny, three-room home. It was a hot summer and I remember doing dozens of cloth diapers in an ancient spin washer. I had no dryer. As I hung them on the line, I wondered, "How will I handle this in the winter?"

One scorching summer day, my mom's car rolled up the driveway. Grandma was moving and insisted that my little family live rent-free in her home—right across from my parents. My mom *informed me,* "I'm going to babysit. You're going back to school in two weeks, so you better get packing!"

"Yes, Ma'am!" I was never so happy with Mom telling me what to do.

Back on Track

It was a win-win for everyone. I went to school, Mom raised my son during the day. My very domestically inclined mom baked cookies and cakes with my son in tow. She did crafts and paintings with him, took him swimming, and made snowmen. I spent my evenings and weekends with my little family. It was a very happy time for all of us.

We convinced the school principal to allow me directly into Grade 11 with my peers, skipping Grade 10 altogether. It was during this time I became interested in computers, business, machines, typing and office administration. I went on to complete all the accounting courses early. To keep me busy, I was entrusted to work in the school office copying, filing and answering the phone. The universe was providing for me.

Opportunities for me as a teen mom were landing in my lap at a furious pace. I won several cash bursaries, plus a four-year scholarship. My entire college education, books and all, was provided, right before my very eyes. I was going to college—*in the BIG CITY!*

I spent the next few years alternately attending college and working a coveted co-op position in a public accounting office. I was given preference as a young mom. The experience was invaluable: personal taxes, bookkeeping, financial statement preparation, and access to cutting edge computer software. Life was great on the career front and the future was looking good.

At the same time, my personal life was on the downslide. My happiness at college and meeting new people brought intense tension at home and our relationship deteriorated. We split. I was both devastated and relieved that it was over. The migraines stopped. I was released from that prison of making myself small, of being less than my full potential in order to please someone else.

Three years later, at age 22, I married the son of a minister. The following year our beautiful daughter was born. My career as an Office Manager was looking good. I loved the job and worked with the owners to help grow their two industrial companies. I started my first bookkeeping and tax company, serving clients in retail and manufacturing. It was a period of great satisfaction and growth.

By the time I was twenty-five, our thriving life took a turn for the worse. On maternity leave with my youngest child, my husband was laid off his construction job. The housing market in Kelowna crashed overnight.

Over the next three years, we experienced the ups and downs of being a young married couple. We were desperately broke and raising three young children. We moved several times, eventually settled in Calgary.

Upon arrival, my greatest opportunity was at a company that to this day, I love dearly. I continued my personal development journey, but as I grew and changed, the environment felt increasingly toxic and draining. I had to leave. It was a familiar pattern I began to see in my life.

As the company educated me, I had many plans for business improvement. They would come in floods after a course or seminar and I would happily spill the ideas onto the management team. I gushed with excitement and enthusiasm for making upgrades to "our" business.

My suggestions, however, were met with, "We can't do that," or "We don't need that." This was a trigger reminiscent of childhood when I was told to have "realistic expectations" and dumb myself down—to once again, make myself small and get into the box.

Oh, the lessons I learned! I realize my greatest learning was not in formal training, but on the front lines of a corporation, in the trenches of managing a large company with my comarades.

I muddled my way through the only way I knew how. I created bonds and relationships, informal lines of communication. I built a team and a network.

A New Kind of Classroom

I learned a lot about people during this time. This deepened my interest and need to learn about personalities and influences. I wanted to learn about leadership styles, management theories and practices, and study great world leaders.

As I studied, I noticed patterns of behavior passed down through the generations of business leaders; some good, some bad. Because these cycles may occur over long periods of time, they can be misread or go unnoticed, especially when personal power or strong emotion is involved. Building awareness around these patterns and cycles is a major key in turning obstacles into opportunities.

While I studied patterns of the great leaders, I was simultaneously blind to a pattern in my own life—the pattern of toxic relationships. I was too closely involved to recognize it. My marriage plummeted over several intense issues. How to make it work became the biggest mystery for me to solve. I feared rollercoasters and was certainly unprepared for one I had no idea I was on.

Soul-sucking, rollercoaster relationships are a place where our greatest strengths can become our greatest weaknesses. I was strong. I made impossible situations work—personally and professionally. The cycles of living with toxic relationships were in full swing in all aspects of my life.

At work, I could wear my smiling face, be compliant, and do my best to make situations work. I was paid to do this, and we needed the paycheque.

On the home front, life was inconsistent and unpredictable. We couldn't seem to break unhealthy patterns and we briefly separated.

After several more months of trying to make our marriage work, and as the toxic cycle continued to spin, a breakthrough occurred. As I focused on myself, the pattern returned in full force, stronger than ever.

I knew I had to break it.

Freedom

I opened up with someone I could trust. For once I was honest about my pain, the endurance of the stress, and having to constantly walk on eggshells in my relationship. Something clicked inside me. My strength increased. Instead of "making it work," I focused on knowing how and when to make the cycle *stop.*

As I went through a difficult divorce, adversity intensified and continued. But it brought about something powerful. I had changed. *My view of myself was different.*

Yes, I was victimized, but I refused to be a victim any longer. I took 100% responsibility. I reclaimed my power. I alone was in charge of how long to hold on to the anger, the pain, the hurt, and how deep I would allow the impact to go.

It is said that holding onto anger and vengeance is like drinking poison, hoping the other person will die. I have since gone through the process of releasing the stranglehold my emotions had on me for so many years. This significant decision gave me the power to change my life and escape the prison walls that held me back..

Wisdom from the School of Hard Knocks

Be – Do – Have

I began the process to BE the kind of person I needed to be, to DO the kind of things I needed to do, in order to HAVE what I wanted to have.

I became aware that the true nature of my incarceration was not solely the system design, but that of my own thinking. *I was buying into the idea that I had to wait to be happy.*

I had it backwards. I was waiting to HAVE the right circumstances: for the magic number, enough money in savings, the right house, the right car, the right relationship. I was waiting to be happy. I was waiting to be who I really wanted to be.

My own thinking was keeping me trapped. As I processed through the events of my life, I found this self-imprisonment pattern. The walls constructed of people-pleasing, other's expectations, false beliefs, and fear were kept secure behind a door of denial.

There were many prisons I constructed:

- Being overweight
- Being addicted to cigarettes and food
- Compromising myself for attention and love
- Staying in an abusive marriage and employment situation.

I kept myself in these prisons waiting to HAVE, instead of BE. I buried the keys, along with my self-worth and self-esteem. I buried them under mountains of someone else's values and expectations. I buried my dreams, while selling myself to others to feel needed, wanted and loved.

I had buried ***me***!

Who do you need to BE, to DO the things you need to do, in order to HAVE the life YOU want to have?

The Saucer and the Cup

Imagine a beautiful gold-rimmed teacup, the ones with the little matching saucers your grandma used to bring out for special gatherings. Imagine tea being poured into the cup. It is so delicious and aromatic! You share some with everyone. You share, and share until there is nothing left—for anyone, yourself included.

As an over-giver and rescuer—YOU are the *empty* cup.

Now imagine the same scenario where tea is poured and the cup overflows. With delight, you share with everyone you love—but only from the saucer. Overflowing with deliciousness and love, the cup remains full. And as more tea is added to the cup, more overflows into the saucer and there is more to give.

As a person who cares for and loves themselves first—YOU are that *full* cup.

I was on a path to burn out. This illustration literally saved my life. The universe is a kind and gentle leader for me. It pointed me in the direction of the personal development world, with huge splashes of self-care and spirituality. My inner being, my spirit, was calling out to me to be nurtured.

Personal development does this for me. It feeds my spirit and allows me to choose what I allow into my life. I now choose my influences. I now choose my practices.

I chose to stop giving from my spiritual cup until it was empty. I began to fill myself up, becoming healthier and stronger. As I nurtured my own spirit, I found I had more to give to other people. And I had more to give to myself.

I married a wonderful man named Trevor, and he and I have chosen the personal growth journey together. We have had many ups and downs, both personally and in our marriage. He helped me raise the kids into amazing adults. We now have grandchildren! Our life journey has not always been smooth, but learning these lessons together helps keep us on the path of *creating* a life and businesses we both *love.*

Express Your Gratitude

The last and most powerful practice I will share with you is to express gratitude. It makes you feel richer, abundant, happier, even more confident. What you focus on expands! Think of all you have, instead of what is missing.

Consider your:

- Relationships
- State of health
- Ability to perceive and think
- Material goods
- Abundant resources
- Education and experiences
- Ability to choose

Have gratitude for yourself in achieving a goal, no matter how small. It is not always about the giant win. Acknowledge steps forward, have gratitude for the small things and more will appear.

And Finally, Kiss Your Boss Goodbye!

My personal and business growth led to me quit my high paying job after seventeen years. I'm pursuing the life of my dreams.

It. Is. Happening.

I am building my business with my program, "Kiss Your Boss Goodbye." The program provides online training, group coaching and mentoring for other small business entrepreneurs in transition, still stuck wearing that gleaming set of Golden Handcuffs.

I help people with their own journey—to BE the person they need to be, in order to DO the things they need to do, so they can HAVE what they want to have. I provide training and guidance in areas of marketing, finance, systems, and accountability. I am a mentor with a well-rounded knowledge-base, education, and first-hand experience.

In "Kiss Your Boss Goodbye," we know that who you are personally is the foundation of your business success. We holistically help you to be the best self you can be and teach you the business skills you need. We bolster your strengths to the max, without letting them slip past the tipping point into weakness.

Has your greatest strength ever passed that tipping point?

Some indications:

- What you used to love now feels like a chore.
- You're feeling resentful.
- Your agenda is consumed with other people's problems.
- You give too much unpaid service in your business.
- People call you only when they need something.
- You take on projects to feel needed or get acknowledgement.

When your greatest strength becomes your greatest weakness, it is like driving a car, pedal to the metal, with the handbrake engaged. For a car, this means burning rubber. For you, it means BURN OUT.

The Golden Handcuffs

Culturally, we are taught to sacrifice our present in favor of a future: a fantasy future where we live in peace and happiness, in retirement, on the beach. However, postponing our happiness and fulfillment keeps us in bad jobs, tough situations, and toxic relationships.

These choices hold us prisoner.

If you stay in your job because of the benefits and pension—and you no longer enjoy it;

If you slug your way each day, through traffic, through snow—and you hate it;

If you miss out on every bright sunny day because you are trapped in your cubicle;

If you hang in there, praying for Friday and dreaming of retirement…

These are your Golden Handcuffs. YOU choose how long to wear them.

Free Yourself

For the better part of my adult life, I allowed others to rule over me, my emotional and spiritual needs, my dreams of freedom. I had created my own shackles, held fast by my desire to please everyone *but* myself.

While my journey is far from over, that deep, black hole I felt inside myself as a young teen is now a place bursting with joy, excitement and love—real love—for myself, for those on this journey with me, and for this amazing life I am now finally really living!

You, too, can kiss your boss goodbye and build the life of your dreams!

Release YOUR Golden Handcuffs—you have the keys.

Lessons Learned:

1) The BEING comes before the DOING and the HAVING.
2) Become an expert at recognizing patterns and cycles to reclaim your power.
3) Your biggest strength can become your greatest weakness if not in balance.
4) Give from the saucer, not the cup.
5) Express gratitude for even the smallest of things, and more will appear.

Mindset Tips:

1) You do not have the right mindset yet, or you would already be doing it. Start here.
2) Live your life—on purpose—now.
3) "Stuckness" comes from living someone else's values, someone else's dreams.
4) Events can happen "to" you, or they can happen "for" you. How do you see them?
5) Release the Golden Handcuffs. Let yourself out of the box. You have the keys.

Aha Moments and Self Reflection

Note your Thoughts

Leslie Tremblay

Leslie's ambition and education have been her pathway to achieving a rewarding career as a professional administrator. She is a lifelong learner with an ongoing desire to investigate the more intrinsic qualities in life and what makes us who we become.

She continuously steps outside her comfort zone, both personally and professionally, knowing that this is the only way one grows. Her passions include travel, family, community service, and inspiring others to become better versions of themselves through guidance in personal and professional advancement/ development.

Her greatest accomplishment was at the age of forty-two when she gave birth to her son, Dominic. Leslie never gave up trying to be a mom. Along with her husband, she teaches her son how to become the best person he can be.

Leslie's life is about balance and not giving up on her dreams.

Connect with Leslie:

Lesliert@telus.net

Chapter 12

The Beginning of the Beginning

By Leslie Tremblay

There was no dramatic or tragic story about the end. Nothing about it was messy. We simply drifted apart and became friends more than lovers. This change was sad for both of us, and we knew we deserved more than simply friendship. So, early one January morning, we hugged goodbye, and off he went to start his new life…and I mine.

There I sat in my quiet house, alone and totally lost. I thought to myself, *Who am I? What do I like? Who are my friends?* You see, during my fourteen-year-marriage, I allowed myself to move into his life. His likes became my likes. His friends became my friends. Slowly but surely, I slipped away from all that was mine. I was thirty-seven years old and had lost my identity. It was time to find my unique self.

What is a difficult experience you've been through? How did you handle it? During challenging times, we can choose to either let those circumstances rule us, or we can rule our circumstances. Ultimately, the choice is ours. You've probably heard that a thousand times. Yes, how you deal with life is all about choice, and what you choose to do isn't always easy. I learned to make hard choices easier by having a constant voice in my head tell me, *Today is the first day of the rest of my life, and I choose me. Today's marvelous.* Present tense is the key to this ever so important self-talk.

Have you ever heard the saying, "What you focus on you find"? I am one hundred percent certain this is wholeheartedly true. I'm now at a crossroad, and this is my chance. I can choose to be a victim of my circumstances, or I can be the heroine of my own story. With God's good grace, I choose the latter. This heroine's life is filled with challenges, setbacks, and ultimate wins.

Grief Is a Funny Emotion

Fourteen years with the same person in my life, and now he was gone. I wondered, *How should I feel right now? Should I cry? Should I be angry? Devastated? Happy? Did I try hard enough? Would we still be married if only I had?* What was the right response to these confusing questions? The simple truth is, there wasn't one. My response was different based on the conditions surrounding the end. For me, it was numb, just plain old numbness. I didn't know how to feel.

The Big, Scary, Single World

Heading out into the world of being single was scary and uncomfortable. *How on earth am I ever going to do this?* I wondered. My solution was, each morning, to give myself a pep talk. *Alright lady, let's pull up those big girl panties and get going.* A sense of humor during this new period in my life was an absolute necessity. Making myself 'get out of my box' was uncomfortable, yet also necessary. With these unfamiliar behaviors, I began to flourish and grow. I was determined to find out who this woman was.

The Power of Underwear

Have you heard of the power of underwear? My grandma, bless her soul, would say, "Leslie, if you look good, you feel good." This emerging new woman started with underwear. The first stop was a visit to the local boutique to get a proper fitting. I scoured the store in search of the most fabulous, lacy, sexy set and spent a small fortune. It's the kind of expense that makes you gulp when you hand over your credit card—but it was completely worth the cost. I deserved to feel good. I worked hard to support myself, and this was going to happen.

Dating, Dating, and Dating

I don't care what anyone says, you can mentally prepare all you want, but life doesn't always go as planned. Sometimes for the better, and sometimes not.

First was my Eat, Pray, Love experience and a wonderful introduction back into this strange and fascinating realm of dating. I mean, how hard could this really be? H.A.R.D. I had no idea what I was getting myself into or what the heck I was doing. Learning how to be single and date was a bizarre and awkward process. I didn't know what to do with myself and needed some practice, so I started going out with my single friends on reconnaissance missions to observe. I was the people watcher.

One fateful night, on one of my 'missions', I laid eyes on him. As he walked across the room, all I could think of was, *Wowza*. Tall, tanned, handsome, muscular, nicely dressed, and overall an amazing specimen…or shall I say eye candy at its finest. As the night went on and courage gained, his sexy accent drew me into a stimulating conversation.

By the end of the night, I was asking my girlfriend, "What am I supposed to do with him?" She politely smirked and said, "Take him home." The blood left my face and fear ran through my veins, there was no way I could possibly…Then I did the unthinkable and did *just that*. I took him home.

I told myself, *I can do this one-night-stand thing*. Turns out nope, I couldn't. This beautiful man was eleven years my junior, and he was fun. Soon it was time for the awkward morning good-bye. I thought, *How does this go?* With a silly smile on my face and after a long pause, he asked, "Would you be interested in seeing each other again?" I accepted, of course. We made plans for the following evening, and off he went. As the door closed, I did a silly little dance that may have included a jump or two.

Date night arrived, and I was a wee bit excited. Well, maybe a bit more than wee. As our night carried on, I discovered that he was moving back east. He was finishing his time in the service and heading back home. He was here for three more months. We made a conscious decision to continue to see each other. It was clearly understood there was an expiration date, and we made the most of our precious time.

Those three months went fast, and now it was time for him to go. He kissed me good-bye, and that was that. The fond memories made me smile, but seeing him drive away made me sink a little. The question crept in again, *Now what?* He had so beautifully filled a void for a short period of time, but now I had to settle down and figure out this life of mine.

Distractions

The next few months were filled with busy projects like home renovations and 'shiny object' purchases. I indulged in new furniture, home accessories, and underwear…can't forget the underwear. So much time being spent trying to find just the right piece. Way too much time. These were good distractions, but they were simply distractions. Keeping busy was my excuse for not moving forward.

Back in the Game

What I realized about doing all of this busy work was that I wasn't out meeting people or being as social as I wanted to be. It dawned on me as I watched my favorite program, *Woman, you are never going to meet anyone sitting here alone.* At that very moment, I declared, "I will go out with whomever asks, with no judgment." I really did want a relationship.

As you can imagine, that attitude didn't turn out so well. After several 'interesting' fellas, another revelation hit me. *Why on earth did I think that was a good idea? I would much rather enjoy my own company.* From those experiences, I figured out the type of person I didn't want. Lesson learned.

The Frying Pan Moment

Have you ever gotten to the point of saying, "I now have this figured out" only to realize how incredibly wrong you are? I certainly have, and then it happened. I met a seemingly nice guy, and we hit it off immediately.

He used the right words, talked about meeting his kids, and took impromptu trips out of town. We had the kind of conversations that led me to believe he was interested and invested. Why on earth would he involve his children if he weren't? The behavior I unwisely overlooked included not following through, his belief system and lack of faith, too many "I" conversations, and the weekend disappearances. The 'it feels wrong' sensation was ignored. The gut feeling was that it's not a good fit, but he had so much potential. This is when I should have called it quits. But I told myself, *Hang in there, Leslie. You can help him become a better man.*

You may have heard this before, but you'll hear it from me now. It is not our job to fix anyone. Everyone needs to apply a 'no projects allowed' mindset, period. Lesson learned.

Getting back from his work one weekend, I was waiting for him to pick me up for our pre-arranged dinner. He was unusually late, so I called. Dinner wasn't going to happen. He said, "I'm tired and don't feel like going out." I said, "I understand. You've had a long weekend. Get some rest. I'll talk to you tomorrow." I felt disappointed and went about my night doing laundry and tidying up while listening to some good music.

About an hour later, I heard a knock at the door…it was him. He entered and closed the door. Instead of coming up to greet me, he just stood there. I was surprised, and then slowly descended the stairs. I didn't expect to hear his cold, hurtful words. "I've been away at work and didn't miss you. This relationship won't work for me." In shock, I asked, "Is there someone else?" He said "no," and walked out the door.

I had fallen for the guy and emotionally invested myself. It was brief and but a sliver of time in my life. What started quickly ended just as suddenly. Poof, "This won't work for me," he's gone, and the insecurity tapes play again.

This is what I refer to as my frying pan moment. The moment of utter disbelief and feeling like I'd been hit by a frying pan. *I…can't…breath.* The wind was knocked out of me. I was shock and fell to my knees. The hysterical ugly cry set in. I asked, "What the hell is wrong with me? Why didn't he want me?"

How is it that the pain that came over me was so much more than when my fourteen-year-marriage ended? I had invested way too much, way too fast.

Picking Up the Pieces

I was in an emotionally dark place and felt like the world had fallen from under my feet. I didn't know I could hurt that badly. I so desperately wanted a relationship to work that I overlooked my own values. The old pattern of losing my identity had repeated.

Thank God for amazing friends and family that helped me navigate through the treacherous waters of recovery. I tried hard to take the higher ground and wanted to wish him well. But to be honest, I wanted him to suffer. Revenge and bitterness was a horrible feeling, and I knew I could react better than that. I had to change my attitude and outlook if I was going to grow through my experience in a healthy way.

I was drawn to a little voice in my head that I had heard before. This time I finally listened. *Go to church. Stop trying to do this all yourself. Quit trying to be so strong, and just give your problems to me.* I talked to a friend, and off we went to church.

I was welcomed with open arms and open hearts. I could feel their love. I was truly amazed that the message delivered that day was exactly what I needed to hear. I cried during that service and subsequent services for some time. My spiritual awakening had begun.

Vacation Time

This vacation couldn't have come at a better time, and with the best group of ladies, I could have wished for. We were a group of twelve that included my mom, three aunts, and the rest were mom's friends. I was the youngest, and we all fit well together.

Our first two days were spent in Fort Lauderdale, Florida. We enjoyed the sun, sand, shops, and restaurants. We were already in vacation mode before our cruise started. Then off we went to board our ship for the next ten days. Let the fun begin.

Our trip, a Caribbean cruise, was filled with adventure, relaxation, great talks, and good advice from my seasoned lady gang. We visited many islands, and my favorite was Roatan. I learned how to snorkel, kayaked in the ocean, ate like a queen, and was treated so amazingly well…spoiled really. We even got a few marriage proposals from the locals.

This time away refreshed my soul and was exactly what I needed. The trip also piqued my new interest and passion for travel. I used to believe in coincidences, but I don't anymore. We get what we need, at the time we need it.

Mindset Change

All those years I had been looking for external happiness. What I truly needed was to find inner peace, happiness, and feel good about myself.

Choice…such a simple concept. A single word. Yet, it can be so difficult. We ponder. We try to anticipate. We ask ourselves, *Am I making the right choice? What if I've made the wrong one? Do I stay or do I leave? Will these shoes go with my outfit? Why can't I lose weight?* You get the point.

We go through life making choices all day long. Some are easier than others. We often make big choices into mountainous challenges that seem insurmountable. This mindset is fear of the unknown and is where courage comes in. The film *We Bought a Zoo* presents the idea of twenty seconds of courage. Ask, "What's the worst that can happen?" To practice the courage of choice, simply make a choice. Then adjust and re-adjust the results until you get it right. But make a choice.

My choice was a necessary change in mindset. It was time to look within myself to understand my self-worth, value, and increase my confidence. I needed to work through my limiting beliefs, doubts, and fears.

Here We Go Again

It was months before I was ready to try dating again. I wanted a relationship and was not going to let the past dictate my future. I started by thoughtfully making a list of all the qualities I wanted in a man.

When I first became single, I was talked into trying out for a roller derby team. I loved to skate as a little girl, so I thought it would be fun. The skating sure was, I got in great shape, but this whole trying to knock people off their skates was not for me. Especially being on the receiving end. I gave it a good try, but oh, my sore body.

Remember my comment about not believing in coincidences? A friend I met through my roller derby team told me of a new colleague of hers that just moved to the area. She asked, "Do you want to meet him?" Trusting her judgment, I said, "Yes." That meeting led to a new relationship that changed the course of my life in many amazing directions.

When I was married, we wanted children. As the months passed by, I could not get pregnant, and there were lots of tears. After our divorce, he remarried, and his wife became pregnant. I convinced myself that I was somehow broken and not having children was my fault. For years I carried around the belief that I would never have a baby.

My new relationship led to courtship and thoughts of life long commitment. We brought up the children topic, and he wanted kids. I was convinced that I couldn't and was completely upfront and honest with him. We decided to carry on with our relationship, and I would visit my doctor to find out what our options were.

On a warm July day, I nervously met with my doctor. We went through my options and decided that the best course of action was a referral to the endocrine clinic. The appointment was set for

December, but she encouraged us to start trying to see what might happen.

The first week of October, I realized that I was late…really late. Fear of a negative test crossed my mind. I prayed, "Please Lord, not another negative test." I decided to take the pregnancy test early in the morning. Low and behold, it was positive. I went into the bedroom, woke him up on what was his birthday, and told him the good news. He was so excited, he cried. Vulnerability was one of the qualities I wanted in a man; this attribute was on the 'what I want' list I had made months prior.

Due to my age of forty-one, I was referred for a special ultrasound and additional testing. Lying on the bed getting ready for the test, I was apprehensive. I soon felt ecstatic to see there really was a baby and was already eight weeks along. I wasn't broken after all.

Being pregnant was amazing. I am one of the fortunate women who didn't have any sickness. I have great memories, and there were funny stories along the way. I got so huge that strangers asked if I was having twins. I loved every minute of this beautiful experience.

We opted not to have a gender reveal, so a boy or girl would be a surprise. Then one beautiful warm and sunny spring morning, he arrived. It's a boy! After years of heartache, I finally got to be called "Mommy."

It's All Worth It

As painful as the frying pan moment was, it was an event in my life that I'm thankful for. It was a huge, debilitating lesson that led me to where I am now. I'm in a fulfilling relationship, and we have a beautiful, amazing son.

Life is by no means perfect. It's perfectly imperfect with more work to do on self-development. Personal growth is a lifelong activity, and I strive to be smarter than when I woke up each day, and better than the day before. Our handsome little man looks up to me. I want to be the best version of myself for my family, but most importantly for me.

In the end, people who enter our life do so for two purposes. They teach us a lesson or grace us with blessings. I go to bed grateful and wake up grateful to God for guiding me to exactly where I am in this very moment. Days can be challenging. It's not easy juggling parenting, relationships, career, and self-care. Yet all of these experiences make me the unique individual I am today.

Some valuable lessons I've learned along the way:

- My G.A.F.F. (Give A F#ck Factor) has been significantly adjusted.
- It's okay to say no.
- If you don't ask, the answer is always no. Lean into that discomfort; you'll never know if you don't ask.
- You don't have to go it alone; it's okay to ask for help.
- Courage to ask for what you want is a necessity.
- Listen to your gut. If it walks like a duck and quacks like a duck, it's probably a duck.
- I may not be able to control a situation, but I am responsible for my reaction.
- There are three types of people in the world: Ones that like me, ones that don't, and those that are on the fence. The ones that like me have made up their mind. It's not my responsibility to sway the ones on the fence. The ones that don't, well that's none of my business, so move on.

"You either get bitter, or you get better. It's that simple. You either take what has been dealt to you and allow it to make you a better person, or you allow it to tear you down. The choice does not belong to fate; it belongs to you."

-Josh Shipp

Get distracted. Visit your pity party; just don't live there. Fall to your knees, scream, cry, pray, and then get back up, dust yourself off, and go buy the underwear.

Lessons Learned

1) Travel and experience the world even if it's just the world around you. Getting a different perspective puts things into perspective.
2) Be grateful for your experiences, even the hard ones. They are what will propel you to bigger and better things, if you allow them to.
3) Never give up on your dreams. Create goals and actions that will help you get there. Don't forget to do the 'do', wishing will not get you there.

Mindset Tips

1) Listen to your intuition; it will not lead you astray.
2) Have the courage to ask for what you want. Start small and work yourself up to bigger ones. This will give you practice to gather up your courage. It's going to be uncomfortable, but you'll be okay.
3) Most importantly, be kind to yourself. Love yourself through your process. Love yourself through the adversity. Do not give up; this too shall pass.

Aha Moments and Self Reflection

Note your Thoughts

Heather Andrews

Visibility strategist, publisher, and 6x international bestselling author, Heather Andrews helps her clients share their story with the world by publishing their works online and offline. Heather believes we all have a story to share to help inspire other by publishing their works in books and podcasts.

With her publishing company, and podcast agency, Tenacious Living, she has published over 80 authors in one year and interviewed over 60 individuals to be seen and heard with the power of their story.

As a speaker, Heather inspires audiences by sharing her challenges and the survival strategies that continue to help her optimize adversity. Being a voice in self-discovery and revitalization, she is making a positive difference. She believes in the power of reinvention and helps inspire others to do the same.

Connect with Heather:

Heatherandrews.press

Followitthrupublishing.com

Chapter 13

The Day I Found Out Why

By Heather Andrews

"The two most important days in your life are the day you are born and the day you find out why."

Reverend Ernest T Campbell, 1970

The day I found out I had been "restructured" out of my life-long healthcare career was devastating. I was totally at a loss as to what to do and paralyzed with fear in the face of the unknown. I had worked hard for the better part of twenty years, climbing the corporate ladder until I got my *dream job*.

For the first time in my adult life, I was unemployed. I was angry, relieved, and scared all at the same time. When I broke the news to my family, I felt like a failure. My self-worth was smack-dab at the bottom of a perpetually flushing toilet. I was hanging on by a thread, but I was more afraid of staying in a slump, than of moving forward without having all the answers.

I knew in my heart of hearts this was happening for a reason, I just didn't know what it was at the time. I knew I was never going back to healthcare management. This career break was the impetus for change—I just didn't quite comprehend how grand that change would be, or where it was going to take me.

Twenty days later, I was back at work as a front-line healthcare worker. I also enrolled in a mentorship coaching program. I was a mentor to many in my previous role, so why not choose coaching as a business venture?

As the months followed one another around the sun, my business sprouted and grew from a boutique independent coaching service, to being asked to participate in a co-authored book, to speaking engagements.

In early 2017, my publisher and mentor, Kate Batten, took me under her wing and pointed me in the direction of becoming a publisher myself. It seemed the world was crying out for healing and the way to do that was through an age-old process—power of story.

The Reinvention of Heather Andrews…as Heather Andrews™

Up until that point, I still struggled to really to *believe* in my own story, to believe myself. I struggled to find my purpose, my new identity, *my why*.

And then it happened: the day that changed everything.

I remember that day vividly; that monumental moment when *everything* clicked, and everything changed. On June 7 2017, *Obstacles Equal Opportunities*, my first compilation book, launched into the stratosphere. It shot up the Amazon best-seller list, in not *one*, but *three* categories. I was elated! Follow It Thru Publishing was put on the map, and a shiny new division of my company made its way into the world like a rocket.

Since that day, life has ramped up faster than the California Screamin' Rollercoaster at Disneyland. The success that book has brought to all involved is nothing short of phenomenal. We are living 'next level,' and are so excited about everything that is coming up.

But I am here to tell you the obstacles ain't over yet. The challenges are different now. As my company grew in size, so did the obstacles and in some ways they took a different twist. Of course, not all obstacles are bad, most have been good problems to havebut, oh my soul—have they tested me.

I had to ask myself: Are you sure you want this business of yours? What are you willing to do to succeed? What, and sometimes who, are you willing to sacrifice? Most often, I sacrificed time for myself which rippled into time with my family. Even today, as I run this entrepreneurial gauntlet, I am tested repeatedly. But I know without a doubt, as I sit here writing this today, I wouldn't take a different route. This journey is only getting bigger and better! It's absolutely *fking amazing*—and I don't use that word lightly.

Growing my business is truly the most rewarding thing I have ever done. It's also the hardest thing I have ever done. Since that best-seller moment in June 2017, I have overcome more obstacles on the path to greatness than I ever thought possible.

Once I made the decision to go 'all in' with my publishing company, I had to get visible and grow. There was no room for fear or ego as we took the stage, literally, in October 2017 to promote the next compilation project. I started speaking at events to promote the new division of my company. Some events I had to pay to be part of, others were free, and all were great places to practice.

Through stage time, features in magazines and being interviewed on podcasts, Follow It Thru Publishing was becoming increasingly more visible. When you are publishing, you simply can't do it all yourself. Experts are needed, like professional editors and graphic designers to support you. I also hired Jenna Carelli and her agency who helped me market and rebrand as Heather Andrews. Me? A brand? Who would have thought that could happen! It was the antithesis of losing my identity in 2015 due to job restructuring. *This* was a moment that shifted everything in my company.

You Can't Be a Secret and a Success at the Same Time

As we rolled over into 2018, things ramped up very quickly. I had met some influential people through mutual connections, and I was invited to speak on a stage with Dr. John

DeMartini in my hometown of Calgary, Alberta that April. It was a dream come true, yet I was petrified to speak. *Who was I to teach anyone about publishing and the power of story?*

I hired a speaking coach to help me. I felt I had some mental blocks around my own story. My story was unique. More importantly, it was *my* story and I had the ability to empower and inspire others with it. While I can now confidently say I am an expert in my industry, there are still pieces I am learning.

In the same timeframe, I purchased a podcast platform, the Tenacious Living Network. The *Heather Andrews Show* was born. I interviewed over 60 authors/co-authors on my show that year, raising their profiles and increasing their visibility. The podcast series was a game changer in terms of my speaking ability, brand clarity, and business alignment. It also increased my Google search presence to the top of the natural rankings.

All of this led to more speaking opportunities, which in turn, led to more clients for our very small team. The previous owner of the podcast network, Carrie-Ann Baron, stayed on as my business manager to help through the transition. Little did she know what she was in for. She has become a major part of my management team as we tripled in size in March 2019.

In July 2018, we published a book by a business coach on the topic of surviving the first five years in your own business. The key message in her work is that business owners should know their financial numbers. Coming from a lifelong career in government-run healthcare to running a sky-rocketing business, I had to be honest with myself. I did not know my numbers.

My business was at a very pivotal point. Not enough clients could make me go out of business, but too much growth without a large enough team to support clients could be just as detrimental. Not knowing my numbers put my business in crisis. I had to re-finance, moving money around to continue to fund the company. By October, we had consolidated everything with a new slate of repayment plans. In some cases, the opportunity can also create obstacles!

The Big Pivot

As in any January, life was full of resolutions as we rang in the New Year. My resolution was to get a handle on my numbers: budgets, costs, forecasting, expenses and profit margins. I had been undercharging, and I had no buffer for when things went wrong. I choked down thousands of dollars in bad debts, increasing my personal debt load.

What's worse, I was not paying *myself,* as I felt like I had to pay my dues or something to gain the credibility. This is what can happen when the universe hands you an opportunity. I did not have a contingency plan for these obstacles, but I have certainly learned some significant lessons.

My personal strengths, my zone of brilliance, is that I connect with people and show them the power of their own story. I have strong project management skills, and people trust me to help them become the best-selling authors they dream of being. I am a natural at speaking in front of large crowds of people and I know how to inspire and empower others to tell their own stories. I'm great at helping clients get through their fears, reinventing their lives in ways most only dream of and never achieve.

But in terms of business finance, I simply did not know what I did not know. Lesson learned.

In February 2019, I spoke a conference in Tampa, FL. It was more significant than I even know at this point, but what I did learn is that we could not accept any clients for two months as we were wait-listed. It was either we wait or we grow. I will choose growth every time. I put out the hiring call on Facebook, and the team came. We interviewed and found the right souls to coach, edit, guide and support our clients. We have new systems in place, processes for tracking our client's success, and contingency plans for when obstacles inevitably arise. And my numbers and forecasts have never been better.

Today, Spring 2019: in retrospect, I birthed an empire. We have created a North America-wide team, developing opportunities for entrepreneurs, editors, designers, connectors, and collaborators. This community of experts exists for the sole purpose of supporting our authors as they take that giant leap of faith and share their stories with the world.

The numbers are the truest reflection of our efforts. After our Fall 2018 event, from October through December, we signed 37 new clients up for our services and kicked-off their projects. In one year, we grew by 95%, published 85 best-selling Amazon co-authors, 12 books and interviewed over sixty individuals on podcasts and internet radio, and engaged with a multitude of like-minded people speaking on multiple stages in the US and Canada.

Recently, Dr. Erin Oksol and I joined forces to hold our first global event, *Follow It Thru to the Amped Life*. Sixty beautiful souls came together to learn how we embraced who we are and how we overcame our personal and business obstacles. We taught them how to get through the obstacles in their own lives with the power of their own story. It was a dream come true for both of us.

And We're Just Getting Started

The last words of my chapter in Obstacles Equal Opportunities, *Volume 1*, were:

> *The journey isn't over. No way. I'm so driven to get to the next level that I can be a bit impatient along the way. Sometimes I'm curious about whether I'm really making the right decisions. There are days when frustration wins out over optimism, but I don't get stuck in that place anymore. I know how to keep moving. Heather Andrews isn't a job title. I stand for the opportunity to live a better life. I am all about integrity, self-respect and finding value in one's self. I know who I am and I'm fully at peace with Heather.*

The journey is definitely not over and the obstacles will undoubtedly keep appearing as we run the proverbial entrepreneurial gauntlet. We are at another crucial moment in our development as a company, and we have BIG plans ahead.

Here is your cliff hanger:

- In the first quarter of this year, we've already brought on *forty* new clients
- The foundation is set with new support systems in place
- The "Get You Visible" brand has been added, with a group plan being developed

- Monthly events are being planned in different locations across North America
- We're signing on new partners to support growth and increase speaking opportunities
- We're collaborating on *Visibility Strategies for Entrepreneurs* with Jujube Business Builders President, Christopher Darryl
- We are forecast to generate over $1million in revenue this year
- We are starting to plan how to be the next Hay House

At the outset of this chapter, I used the quote:

"The two most important days in your life are the day you are born and the day you find out why."

This quote is often attributed to Mark Twain on social media, but in researching it for this book, it appears that this is likely incorrect. The original quote is attributed to Reverend Ernest Campbell, of New York in the 1970s. However, another version of this famous quote appears in a 1985 publication called, *A Woman & Her Self-Esteem,* by Anita Canfield, which is even more relevant:

"Ask yourself a most profound question: 'What are the two most important days in my life?' The day you were born and the day you find out why you were born!

And why were you born? You were born to bless the lives of others. You were born to make a contribution."

-Mark TwainStudies.com

My wish for you is to ask questions around your obstacles and see what answers come back to you. The obstacle is like a silent whisper to sit up and pay attention to where you're going, to who you are, and to your own 'why.'

Now, I embrace the obstacles, without pity parties, as I know how to lean in to the lesson and ask God: 'What do I need to know to grow?' I believe I am stronger and smarter for what I've learned and that this has galvanized me into a better mentor to others.

For myself, all I can say is I am happy, changing lives and living out a life reinvented. I want the same for you. And remember:

The obstacle is the way.

- Ryan Holiday

Lessons Learned:

1) Resiliency is your best friend once you learn to leave the pity party.
2) When your body is out of sync, the universe will stop it for you if you need to stop.
3) Surround yourself with the right friends, family, team and business partners. You can borrow their belief in you when yours disappears.

Mindset Tips:

1) Stop spinning out of control and listen to your intuition.
2) Believe the obstacle has a lesson *and* see it as an opportunity.
3) Setbacks occur to remind you to look beyond your perception.

Aha Moments and Self Reflection

Note your Thoughts

Conclusion

Now it's your turn!

As we wrap up this journey through Obstacles Equal Opportunities: Volume II, we hope you're already chomping at the bit to get busy. It's time for you to take control of your situation and overcome your own obstacles. The only way past is through.

It's time to put all these strategies, tactics and tools to work for you, as you plot your course around whatever it is that lies in front of you. It's time to reach way down inside of yourself, find your own brand of bravery and jump right in.

It's time to understand that every single obstacle you encounter on your path is a blessing in disguise, and to know that by taking on those challenges with authenticity, vulnerability and positivity, each one is polishing your resiliency until you shine like the diamond I know you are.

It's time to find your own 'why.'

You can't find your 'why' sitting on the couch moping about what hasn't gone right, or simply daydreaming about what your perfect life might look like. Yes, it takes creating a vision, but it also requires a strategy on how to achieve that vision. It takes planning. It takes learning. It takes action. It takes grit to get through the challenges and come out the other side.

And the only way to bring all those things together in one powerful movement is to believe in your own 'why' 110% and go all-in to bring that vision to life.

It's time to dust off your confidence, shake off the negative, be honest and realistic with yourself and really think through how you can overcome adversity in your own life. What tools already exist to help you chip away at that roadblock? Where can you look to find knowledge and training to move yourself to the next level in your evolution? What services can help guide you in the right direction, lighten the load on your own resources, or teach you what you don't know going forward?

The good news is, you don't have to do all this on your own. Many of the co-authors in this book offer services to help you get on your way. Their expert knowledge and experience is there to help you to plot your course, to furnish you with all the tools and strategies you need to help you overcome whatever challenge you're facing, and to advise you of other products and services that may suit your individual business or personal situation.

It's time to be thankful for all you've learned along the way, to find wisdom in lesson, and to change your circumstances by shifting your mindset—and choosing to win from now on.

And finally, it's time to shimmy. Are you ready?

Love,

Heather

Increasing The awareness—The Loss is Real

Pregnancy and Infant Loss Support Centre

By Aditi Loveridge

Did you know that 1 in 4 pregnancies will end in loss?

As you read in my chapter, the journey through pregnancy and infant loss is profound; it is deeply complex. Over the last few years of working within the loss community, I have come to see that not everyone heals in the same way. Yet, there are only a few options of low cost supports available to this community, which I don't think is fair.

The pregnancy and infant loss community deserves to have a space where individuals can come and begin to heal in their own terms and in their own way.

For this reason, I founded the non-profit organization Pregnancy & Infant Loss Support Centre. The Centre is a Calgary based non-profit organization whose mission is to provide free and low-cost access to holistic healing supports for people who might not have otherwise known about, or could afford them—supports that are proven to be pivotal on the path to healing.

We run five peer groups a month and have launched a peer mentoring program so that people who have navigated this complex path can mentor other individuals and families that are new to this journey. This is a deeply, mutually-beneficial program, as it provides mentorship for the newly bereaved, and an opportunity to give back to this community in a meaningful way.

The Pregnancy & Infant Loss Support Centre believes in the power of connection and community. Our centre supports individuals through all stages of loss, and serves as a safe space for individuals of all faiths, ethnicities, sexual orientations, and gender identities who have experienced loss to connect to their community and truly know, see, and feel that they are not alone.

Our services include reiki, coaching, yoga, reflexology, acupuncture, and massage services along with drop-in hours to support individuals in immediate need connection.

We opened in January 2019, and our attendance is increasing every month.

Please follow us on social media at:

www.facebook.com/pregnancyinfantlosssupportcentreyyc

@pregnancylosssupportyyc

If this is a mission you would like to support, contribute to or know someone who could benefit from our services, please contact us at info@pregnancylosssupportcentre.com

Or visit our website

http://www.pregnancyinfantlosssupportcentre.com/

Do You Dream of Being a Published Author?

The best part of what I do is bringing people together to write, share, and inspire those that may feel alone or in need of healing. Your story could help to heal others.

My team will guide you through the writing process, so your idea can become a reality to be shared on worldwide distribution channels.

A book has been referenced as an authority piece for centuries and is known to be one of the best ways to gain instant credibility and visibility with clients in the online and offline space.

If you have a story to share and want to become a published author or co-author in a collaborative, then let's talk.

Book your complimentary call with me.

https://followitthru.as.me/tellyourstory

Here's to your story and someone waiting to read it.

Heather

https://www.facebook.com/groups/GetYouVisible/